REMEMBERING THE TRAUMA

AND HEALING IT

WITH THE TRAUMA OF CHANGE SYSTEM™

RENÉE D. CHARLES, PH.D.

REMEMBERING THE TRAUMA

Copyright © 2018 by Renée D. Charles, Ph.D. All rights reserved.

It is in no way legal to reproduce, duplicate, or transmit any part of this document in any form by any means—electronic, mechanical, photocopy, recording, or otherwise—without prior written permission from the publisher, except as provided by United States of America copyright law.

Unless otherwise noted, all Scripture quotations are taken from the King James Version®. Copyright © 1982 by Thomas Nelson. Used by permission. All rights reserved.

Scripture quotations marked NKJV are taken from the New King James Version®. Copyright © 1982 by Thomas Nelson. Used by permission. All rights reserved.

Scripture quotations marked NIV are taken from the Holy Bible, New International Version®, NIV®. Copyright © 1973, 1978, 1984, 2011 by Biblica, Inc.™ Used by permission of Zondervan. All rights reserved worldwide www.zondervan.com. The "NIV" and "New International Version" are trademarks registered in the United States Patent and Trademark Office by Biblica, Inc.™

Editing by Inksnatcher
Cover design by Emily Jones

Visit the author's website at www.drreneedcharles.com

Library of Congress Cataloging-in-Publication Data:

An application to register this book for cataloging has been submitted to the Library of Congress.

ISBN: 978-1-7338174-0-0

This book contains the opinions and ideas of its author. The information provided in this book is for educational purposes only and should not interfere with current or future relationships with healthcare providers or legal counsel. Under no circumstances will the publisher be held legally responsible or blamed for any reparation, damages, suffering, or monetary loss due to the information herein, either directly or indirectly.

People named in this book are not real. Names and details of their stories have been changed to protect their privacy. Any similarity between the names and stories of individuals described anywhere in this book and individuals who are known to readers is purely coincidental. The narratives are derived from actual patients the author has encountered as a licensed professional therapist. They have granted their express permission to publicize aspects of their experience.

Trauma narratives are shared to contextualize the meaning of trauma, deliverance, and recovery.

Reading these trauma narratives may elicit an emotional response in some readers and re-traumatize those with a history of post-traumatic stress disorder (PTSD). Therefore, caution is advised. Reading the narratives is the sole and utter responsibility of the reader.

Each case narrative described in this book is its own unique set of circumstances. The diagnosis ascribed or inferred to the various narratives is individualized and may not apply to your specific situation.

I have chosen to adopt Bishop T. D. Jake's position to not capitalize "s" in the spelling of the name of satan out of a lack of respect for him.

18 19 20 21 22 — 987654321

Printed in the United States of America

Endorsements

Trauma plagues the body of Christ and the world in general, but the conversation on this topic is limited and diluted. Much dysfunction parades in believers lives due to this travesty. In this book, Dr. Charles calls for a mental reset to help each person live their lives to the utmost.

This uniquely written book merges academic depth alongside biblical truth to help readers receive implicit deliverance. Charles thoroughly unearths how memories, wounds, and bruises can change the trajectory of one's life via their brains. The case studies included add further validity and autoethnographic perspectives of this manuscript.

This book would fare well in various academic and religious settings. Christian counselors and believers alike should indeed add this to their canon of literature.

Alexis Maston-McClinton, Ph.D.

Remembering the Trauma by Dr. Renée D. Charles, Ph.D. is the most comprehensive and detailed study of the traumatic wounds of the soul and body, written from a biblically sound and physiological position of deliverance and healing.

I have longed for such a well-written, balanced teaching in this area for years. Being a seasoned forty-year veteran of deliverance and healing ministry, I recognize and welcome this sound teaching on the damaged emotions, biblically taught in a balanced manner.

This book is an excellent tool for the local church and Christian counselors. It will safely bring healing insight and deliverance to so many who are suffering from trauma and afraid to see the need for both biblical and physiological in-sight.

Apostle Dr. Ivory Hopkins, a.k.a. The General of Deliverance
Overseer and Founder of Pilgrims Ministry of Deliverance
Georgetown, Delaware 19947

Post-Traumatic Stress Disorder (PTSD) develops in response to disruptive external experiences that create deep emotional wounds inflicted by the environment onto the mind, body, and soul. In *Remembering the Trauma*, Dr. Renée Charles proposes a treatment model that incorporates clinical research with biblical truths. This model holds strong potential to empower healing by creating a union of evidence-based practices to rewire the brain with faith-based beliefs that bring a deeper meaning to the process of surviving trauma. This is a must-read for practitioners who incorporate faith-based interventions with therapeutic skills as well as secular therapists seeking to understand better and treat the Christian community.

Donna Simons LCSWR, CASAC

Contents

Endorsements v
Foreword by Dr. Cindy Trimm ix
Author's Note xi
   Ecumenical Leaders, Practitioners, & First Responders xii
Acknowledgments xiii
Prologue 1
   Hijacking the Soul 2
   The Tabernacle 5
   Defining Trauma 7
   Demonic Squatters 10
   The Redemptive Work Continues 10
Chapter 1: Trauma, Memory, and the Vicissitudes of Life 13
   Two Storages of Memory 13
   Traumatization 15
   High-Risk Behaviors 16
   Mislabeling Maladaptive Behaviors 16
Chapter 2: Algorithms, Codes, and Data Files 19
   The Body's Command Center 19
   How Does the Brain Work? 26
   The Mind Shapes the Brain 28
   Triggers and Automatic Responses 35
Chapter 3: Taxonomies of Traumas 35
   Trauma Taxonomies 36
Chapter 4: Trauma and Self-Worth 47
   Levels of Self-Consciousness 47
   Ego States 47
   The Child View 48
   Characteristics of Events That Can Lead to Trauma 50
   Trauma Symptoms 51
Chapter 5: Trauma Wounds 53
   Injury 53
   Abrasions and Internalized Anger 54
   Incisions and Betrayal Trauma 55
   Lacerations and Soul Ties 55
   Puncture Wounds and Childhood Abandonment 55
   Avulsions and Sexual Abuse 56

Chapter 6: Natural and Spiritual Portals **57**
    Spiritual Portals 58
    The ACE Pyramid 60
    Evicting Demonic Squatters 61

Chapter 7: Trauma Bruises: Guilt and Shame **63**
    Guilt..63
    Shame 64
    Trauma Bruising of the Soul 65

Chapter 8: Deliverance, Healing, and Recovery **69**
    Deliverance 71
    The Trauma of Change System Model 74

Chapter 9: Healing Trauma Wounds and Bruises **79**
    The Decision Is Yours...80
    The Four Phases of Physical Wound Healing 80
    Healing Disease and Recovering from Illness 82
    Decreasing the Impact of Trauma 83
    The Trauma of Change System Model – Wound Triage Treatment 84

Chapter 10: Rewiring the Brain **91**
    The Process 91
    The Triune Mind 92
    Neuroplasticity 94
    The Trauma of Change System Model..96
    David: A Biblical Example of Rewiring Your Brain in Faith 99

Chapter 11: The Altar **101**
    Steps of Faith 101
    The Trauma of Change System Model: Recovery Processing Stage 103

Chapter 12: The Final Word **105**
    A Word to Practitioners 105
    A Word to Trauma Conquerors 105
    A Word to the Helpers...105
    A Word to Clergy 106

Appendix 1: ACE Screening **107**
    Adverse Childhood Experience (ACE) Questionnaire 107

Appendix 2 : ACE Screening Score Results **110**

Appendix 3: Prayer of Petition by Evangelist Renée D. Charles .. **111**

Appendix 4: Deliverance Declaration **113**

Appendix 5: How to Close All Doors to Satan **115**

About the Author **119**

Endnotes **120**

Foreword
by Dr. Cindy Trimm

I believe everyone would benefit from reading *Remembering the Trauma*. The very title issues a remarkable challenge to unpack and process the trauma that many have experienced.

Having an extensive background in psychotherapy and being a minister for over forty years, I have counseled and prayed for thousands of people suffering from psychological and spiritual wounds as well as demonic complications. I have reveled in the deliverance and healings I've been privileged to observe. I have seen the usefulness of counseling along with its limits. Counseling helps to develop coping skills but usually does not help the traumatized to become free, so I have a strong desire to read books like this one which discuss the amazing transformation that can come through the combination of therapy techniques, deliverance, and an understanding of the mind-body-brain connection.

Trauma happens to us all—friends, colleagues, families, and neighbors. The Centers of Disease Control and Prevention reports that one in five Americans was sexually molested as a child, one in four has been beaten by a parent to the point of a significant mark being left on their body, and one in three couples engages in physical violence. Twenty-five percent of the population grew up with alcoholic relatives, and one out of eight saw their mother being beaten or hit.[1]

These statistics show us that *Remembering the Trauma* is not only relevant to the world at large but it is also an important resource for the church as God's representative on the earth and in bringing healing to its own population of traumatized people it must contend with. In fact, trauma is so prominent in the Christian community that you can

---

1   V. J. Felitti, Relationship of childhood abuse and household dysfunction to many of the leading causes of death in adults. *The Adverse Childhood Experiences (ACE) Study* (1998), 14(4):245-58.

practically feel its weight on the people who gather during services. Shattered relationships and broken dreams have hurled many into the twilight of their own despair. In the darkness of our personal agony, many scramble for the light but often come up wanting and destitute.

The foundation of *Remembering the Trauma* teaches us that when we understand how trauma works, and when we exercise our option to rewire the brain, we become endowed with a truth that has exceptional power and we can seize opportunities to exit our pain. We come to understand that our distress has an expiration date if we know how to acquire the help we need. The book directs us out of our pain in a masterful style that incorporates her Trauma of Change model, which is woven within the fabric of this book along with the proper interpretation of Scripture and deliverance concepts.

When we have been down and out, we need hope and strategies—this is what this book gives. *Remembering the Trauma* is a powerful tool presented in a strikingly clear way that helps us see that we can finally embrace a more complete vibrant life beyond the pain.

This timely work has the potential to see thousands of lives reclaimed, changed, and extracted from the grip of the enemy and any imposed limitations because of the profound insights articulated here.

Dr. N. Cindy Trimm

Life-Strategist, Author, Humanitarian

Author's Note

The nexus between healing, deliverance, and recovery is a dynamic one that requires a dual focus to eradicate the memory of traumatic events and to set at liberty them that are bruised.

People who have been traumatized hold an implicit memory of traumatic events in their brain and body. The trauma of childhood neglect, abandonment, rejection, betrayal, and sexual abuse, among other traumatic events, can wreak havoc in our bodies and create strongholds in one or more of its ten systems.

Behind every stronghold, a framework of trauma incapacitates unbelievers and believers alike. The spirit of trauma strangles people with feelings of shame and guilt about their past and present lives, which hinders their ability to manifest the glory of God—even after accepting Christ as Lord and Savior.

Deliverance and healing begin initially in the human mind. Jesus asked the man at the pool of Bethesda if he wanted to be made whole. This inquiry points to the first-stage processing phase of healing described in the Trauma of Change System Model. The very act of deciding is neurotechnology.

Deliverance and healing are both restorative processes involving the regaining of possession or control of something stolen to the former and better state of wholeness. Deliverance deals with being liberated from demonically caused mental and physical conditions.

Neuroscience is the scientific study of the nervous system, brain, spinal cord, and related structures. Brain research lets us know that "the brain takes the shape the mind rests upon."[1] The brain is an organ, but the mind is not. The mind is a vessel in which electronic impulses that create thought are contained. Where the mind goes, the body follows.

Trauma affects the brain circuitry, leaving victims of trauma disabled, often with terrorizing memories. The devil seeks to seduce and corrupt the mind. The Word of God tells us that we can retrain our mind and admonishes man to be "transformed by the renewing of your mind."

The good news is, according to neuroplasticity research, one can rewire the brain and rebuild areas affected by trauma. Trauma healing and recovery is an evolving process that is affected by the optimization of brain function, cultural norms, health beliefs, and behavioral codes.

I curated the Trauma of Change System Model (TOC) and introduced the TOC model in the book along with a companion self-help workbook. The Trauma of Change System Model is a Christian-based recovery model that integrates the best of neuroscience, neuroplasticity, psychology, physiology, neuro-theology, and spiritual states of deliverance, healing, and recovery.

By leveraging evidence based neuroscience strategies, coupled with the Word of God, victims of trauma can rewire their brain, develop new mental maps, improve higher-order brain activity, and experience rapid recovery from the spirit of trauma.

Ecumenical Leaders, Practitioners, & First Responders

Remembering the Trauma can serve as a useful resource for many. Often those in ministry and the caregiving field lack an in-depth understanding of the effects of trauma or repeated traumatic experiences on the human body and mind.

I believe the information outlined in the faith-based stage processing recovery system will aid ecumenical leaders, first responders, prophetic ministers, neuroscience coaches, friends, and family members.

Moreover, licensed trauma-informed professionals will learn how to merge neuroscience and biblical spirituality; and gain understanding of the role culture plays in trauma healing and how to advance wound healing.

Applying the knowledge and techniques shared in *Remembering the Trauma*, we can each be better equipped to meet the needs of this unique population and minister more effectively to those whose core beliefs about their safety, self-worth, and purpose are in doubt because of the spirit of trauma.

Acknowledgments

I want to express my gratitude to my friends, family, colleagues, and clients, who have supported me during this incredible journey.

A special thanks to Alexis Maston-McClinton, Ph.D., for providing me a platform to present on the topic of trauma memory, healing, and deliverance. It was a privilege to minister alongside Apostle John Eckhardt, Apostle Ivory Hopkins, Apostle Kimberly Daniels, Apostle Travis Jennings, Apostle Alexander Pangani, and Prophetess Sophia Ruffin at the 2016 Generals of Deliverance Conference.

The focus of the Generals of Deliverance Conference was crafted to develop, equip, and position a network of battlefield-ready kingdom defenders in position to dismantle systems within the kingdom of darkness. Dr. Maston-McClinton, through pure creative genius, married the biblical definition of deliverance and healing with neurotheology.

The approach was a one-of-a-kind conference framework, whereby participants not only received training and understanding but also had access to certified, trained behavioral health faith-based care counselors and other medical practitioners.

Jesus came to set the captive free. Each General of Deliverance is serving as an ambassador of the kingdom of God, and carries an apostolic mantel to facilitate deliverance, healing, for victims on the battlefield victimized by the spirit of trauma.

Prologue

In the book of Genesis, God the Father said, "Let Us create man in our image and likeness and make man from the dust of the earth" (Gen. 1:26). It pleased God to make humanity (Adam and Eve) to be in a relationship with Him and with one another.

Within any healthy relationship, mutual trust is supposed to be a nonnegotiable guiding principle. Mankind's relationship with God is no exception. God established parameters with Adam and Eve. He commanded them to not eat from the Tree of the Knowledge of Good and Evil (Gen. 2:9). God trusted a man to obey His command. He sternly warned Adam and Eve they would surely die if they partook of the fruit of the forbidden tree (Gen. 2:17). Satan, an enemy of God, challenged this command and persuaded Eve to eat from the forbidden tree. Satan assured Eve that no adverse consequences would result from acting contrarily to God's Word, and thus, Eve convinced Adam to also eat the fruit of the forbidden tree.

COMMANDS AND CONSEQUENCES

As a result of their disobedience to God's command, Adam and Eve's relationship and trust with God was broken. Their disobedience to God was an outright act of betrayal. By eating from the forbidden tree, they rejected God's authority. Through the violation of one man (Adam), sin, sickness, and death entered the world.

A TRAUMATIC BETRAYAL OF TRUST

Every betrayal of trust is a traumatic violation that results in wounds and bruises. When Adam and Eve sinned, they betrayed God's trust. Both God the Father and Jesus, who is God the Son, understand the pain inflicted by trauma.

Jesus sustained physical, emotional, and spiritual trauma at Calvary. The trauma God the Son experienced at there, where He endured and conquered death, hell and the grave, can serve as a picture of the trauma that often afflicts believers today.

The Bible says in Isaiah 53:5 (NKJV) that Jesus was "wounded for our transgressions, He was bruised for our iniquities; the chastisement for our peace was upon Him, and by His stripes, we are healed."

THE REDEMPTION

Despite Adam's betrayal, disobedience, and rejection of God, God still loved him. God desired to reconcile their broken relationship. Though God once regretted that He made humanity (Gen. 6:8), He never repented of redeeming mankind. Scriptures are replete with passages that reveal God has always loved us and had a plan for us, despite our sins (Jer. 29:11; 2 Cor. 5:21).In His goodness, God strategized a plan to redeem mankind back to fellowship with Himself. God's plan to restore mankind back to a relationship with Him is called redemption.

I envision the Trinity plenary session as God the Father saying, "I will forgive and restore man to my original purpose and relationship with me." Jesus, God the Son, then says, "I will be the ransom to redeem mankind from the curse of sin and death." God the Holy Spirit then says, "Once they are redeemed, I will provide guidance and power to lead them into all truth and knowledge."

Through His perfect obedience, Jesus (who had never sinned) suffered the penalty for the sins of all humanity. The Son gave His life as a ransom to redeem mankind from the curse of sin and death. The selfless sacrifice of Jesus allows us to now enjoy fellowship with God and live eternally with Him.

Hijacking the Soul

The effect of trauma can have a dramatic impact on our bodies and our minds. When there is a traumatic experience, the enemy tries to highjack the soul and the body through demonic attachments. These are dispatched to impede the natural healing process in a person's life by causing emotional reactions that are disproportionate to current events.

THE SOUL KNOWS

To know is a cognitive process and a primary function of the prefrontal lobe of the brain, often referred to as the CEO. There is a difference between the mind and the brain. "The brain takes the shape that the mind rests upon."[1] The brain is an organ made up of physical matter in which the Holy Spirt resides, and the mind is the invisible conscious part that manifests itself as thoughts.

> For the word of God is living and active, sharper than any two-edged sword, piercing to the division of **soul and of spirit**, of joints and of marrow, and **discerning** the thoughts and **intentions of the heart**. (Heb. 4:12 ESV, emphasis added)

Thoughts and the intentions of the heart affirm that the mind is a part of the soul. Proverbs 19:21 and 24:14 indicate that knowledge and wisdom are related to the soul. Proverbs 2:10 says, "Wisdom will enter your heart, and knowledge will be pleasant to your soul." Lamentations 3:20 says, "My soul remembers them well," indicating that the soul can remember things. Psalm 139:14 says, "My soul knows it well." By these verses, we can be safety assume that the mind (soul) is an invisible part of the brain, the organ to know, to consider, and to remember.

THE SOUL WILLS

The second part of the soul is the will. Decision-making is the primary function of the *frontal lobe of the brain*, responsible for higher thought processes associated with planning, decision-making, voluntary muscle movement, processing speech, smell, and emotions.[2]

Scripture provides examples of the will deciding to choose and to refuse. To choose and to refuse are both decisions and functions of the will:

> So that my soul chooseth strangling, And death rather than these my bones. (Job 7:15 ASV)

> My soul refuses. (Job 6:7 ASV)

> Now set your heart and your soul to seek after Jehovah your God. (1 Chron. 22:19 ASV)

> A man's heart deviseth his way: but the LORD directeth his steps. (Prov. 16:9)

THE SOUL HAS EMOTIONS

The third part of the soul is the emotion. Mankind is hardwired with emotions stimulated by environmental stimuli. *Emotions* are lower level responses occurring in the subcortical regions of the brain, the amygdala, and the ventromedial prefrontal cortices, creating biochemical reactions in your body, altering your physical state.[3]

The amygdala (referred to as the emotional brain) is a part of the limbic system discussed further in chapter 3. Its primary role involves the processing of memory, decision-making, and emotional reactions.

Song of Songs 1:7 and Psalm 42:1 are letters born out of the emotions of love and deep feelings. One can safely surmise that to love is a function of the soul.

> On the day of the attack, David said to his troops, "I hate those 'lame' and 'blind' Jebusites. (2 Sam. 5:8 NLT)

> Thus said Hezekiah—A day of distress, and rebuke, and despising is this day; for come have sons unto the birth, and power there is not to bring forth. (2 Kings 19:3 YLT)

Deuteronomy 14:26 and Jeremiah 22:27 reveal that the soul has desires.

> The Lord God says, "I swear, I will let my strong feelings speak for me! I will let Edom and the other nations feel my anger. (Ezek. 36:5 ERV)

Man was made a living soul in the image and likeness of God, who has feelings and emotions.

> For we have not an high priest which cannot be touched with the feeling of our infirmities; but was in all points tempted like as we are, yet without sin. (Heb. 4:15)

Hating, loathing, despising, and love are expressions of emotions found in the soul.

THE SOUL AND SELF-CONCEPT

Self-concept is best understood as a three-dimensional awareness of the self. The soul profoundly affects one's mental map (*self-image*) of how a person sees themselves and the qualities they believe they possess. The value or *level of esteem* you ascribe to yourself is referred to as *self-esteem*. The way you *would like to see* yourself is the aspect of the self-referred to as the *ideal self*.[4]

THE SOUL AND SENSORY MEMORY

Each of the three parts of the soul—mind, will, and emotion—is affected by trauma. Trauma is an offense to the soul and stored as sense memory. Attacks to the soulish realm, such as rape, sexual abuse, or parental rejection, are always imprinted, stored, and processed as sensory memories.

Sensory memories are imprinted and stored by how our five senses were experiencing the trauma at the time it was occurring. They are often retained as negative images, feelings, and sensations stored in various parts of the brain.[5]

Sensory memories are not quickly dispelled or dislodged from the mind by human will. Sensory memories shape our perception of reality, forming the mental map which guides conscious and unconscious behavior. According to quantum physics, in the natural realm our knowledge of reality is limited to our understanding of time, space and matter.[6]

The Tabernacle

God gave Moses divine specifications for building the tabernacle. Many theologians view the structure and design of the temple as an archetype of the human body.

THE ARCHETYPE OF THE BODY TEMPLE

The Old Testament temple according to 1 Kings 5:3–5 and 1 Chronicles 28:2–3, 6, and 10 was made up of three parts: the outer court, the inner court, and the holy of holies and several rooms. God made man in his likeness and image. As the Father, Son, and Holy Ghost are one, so is the temple. The human body likewise has three parts: the physical body, the soul, and the spirit. The physical body can be viewed as the outer court. The soul is considered to be the inner court (with all of its components). The spirit is the sacred place the holy of holies.

The holy of holies is the secret place and throne room of the Most High God (Exodus 19:1). Satan attacks the physical bodies of believers and nonbelievers alike with sickness and diseases to gain access.

TRIPARTITE DIVISIONS OF MAN

God has made all things in threes. Even atoms have three parts: neutrons, protons, and electrons. God created the human brain as vast as the infinity of the universe.[7]

Within the *Spirit of man*, there are three functions of the spirit, governed by the Holy Spirit: 1) the conscience, or to know right and wrong, and when the Holy Spirit convicts of sin, 2) fellowship—to contact and commune with God in praise and worship; and 3) intuition—to receive a direct sense and knowledge from God through wisdom.[8] Intuition is a function of the right hemisphere of the brain and will be discussed further in chapter 3.

Three energetic components comprise the *tripartite divisions of the psyche*, according to Freud's *psychoanalytic theory* of the id, ego, superego. In Freud's theory, the id corresponds to the unconscious, the ego is the conscious, and the superego is the "preconscious."[9]

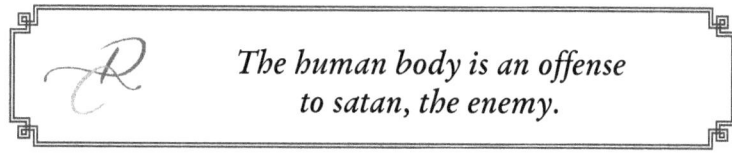

The human body is an offense to satan, the enemy.

The human body has ten essential organ systems: respiratory, digestive, excretory, nervous, endocrine, immune or lymphatic, integumentary (skin and hair), skeletal, muscular, and reproductive.[10] Each system can become affected by the spirit of trauma and be an access portal for inhabitation by demonic squatters.

THE BODY HOUSES THE SPIRIT AND SOUL

Man is a spirit who possesses a soul and lives in a body. The soul is the place of our will, emotions, and intellect. The body is the gateway to the spirit and soul. The human body houses the spirit and soul. "The spirit of man is the candle of the LORD, searching all the inward parts of the belly" (Prov. 20:27).

As a tactical maneuver, satan intends to use trauma to destroy the spirit of man. The spirit is the secret place where we commune with God. satan knows our bodies are the temple of God. He uses trauma to hijack the body and soul to gain entrance or access into the spirit of man.

This emotional reaction to a perceived harmful event, attack, or threat to survival activates a physiological reaction. The physiological reaction that occurs in both your body and brain may result in a variety of unhealthy behavior and personality patterns, compulsions, and addictions.

After the resurrection of Christ, the apostle Paul spoke prophetically to the church at Corinth saying, "Know you not that ye are the temple of God, and that the Spirit of God dwelleth in you?" (1 Cor. 3:16). Paul's inquiry informed the Corinthian church to know that the human body itself is an offense to the enemy.

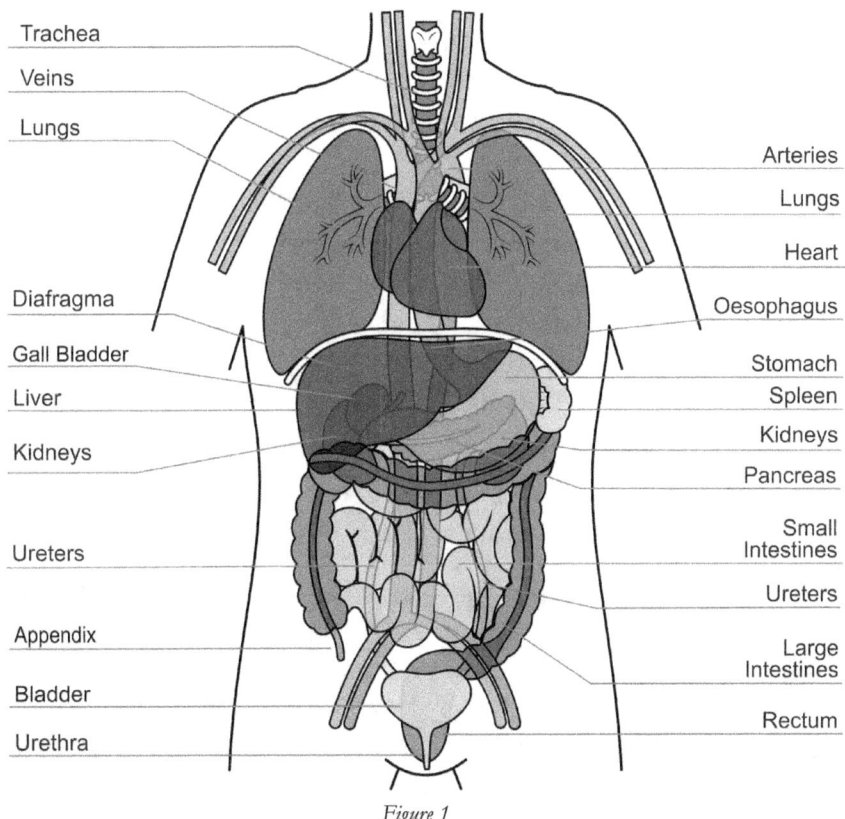

Figure 1

Defining Trauma

Trauma is defined from the Greek word for *wound*. Trauma can also mean "to pierce, damage or defeat."[11] *Individual trauma* is defined as what "results from an event, series of events, or set of circumstances experienced by an individual as physically or emotionally harmful or life-threatening with lasting adverse effects on an individual's functioning and mental, physical, social, emotional, or spiritual well-being."[12] Sigmund Freud defined trauma as "a breach of the protective barrier against stimuli leading to feelings of overwhelming helplessness." While many sources of trauma are physically violent, psychological traumas can have a life altering impact on the victim's mental and emotional stability.

THE SPIRIT OF TRAUMA

There is a violent battle taking place in the spiritual realm. The devil and his angels launch attacks against believers and nonbelievers alike to traumatize their souls. The spirit of trauma is satan's use of traumatic events to wound people, interrupt healthy function, and immobilize both believers and nonbelievers. Satan attempts to use trauma to leave people with deep wounds, knowing the wounded warrior will have a harder time waging war against his kingdom.

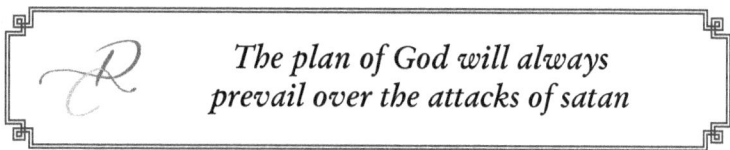

The plan of God will always prevail over the attacks of satan

STATISTICS AND THE SCOPE OF TRAUMA

Trauma appears to be a fact of life. Satan uses evil spirits to exact dimensions of violence, sexual abuse, intimidation, betrayal, abandonment, rejection, sickness, and diseases as traumatic events to impact the soul.

An estimated 70 percent of adults in the United States have experienced a traumatic event at some **point in their lives. Childhood trauma, including abuse and neglect, is recorded as America's single most important** public health challenge. One in five Americans has been molested. One in four grew up with parents who were alcoholics. One in three couples engaged in intimate partner violence.[13]

RAPE

A national survey of four thousand women found that one in eight reported being the victim of forcible rape. On average, twenty-four people per minute are victims of physical violence, including rape or stalking, by an intimate partner in the United States.[14]

"The percentage of women who were raped as children or adolescents and also raped as adults was more than *two times higher* than the percentage among women without an early rape history."[15] Of the number of victims abused, half had been raped more than once, approximately one-third were younger than eleven, and over 60 percent were under eighteen.[16] Victims of the crime of rape are the largest group of people with post-traumatic stress disorder in this country.

CHILD ABUSE

Every day, "children are beaten, burned, slapped, whipped, thrown, shaken, kicked and raped."[17] Most traumas begin at home within the child's caregiving system and include physical, emotional and educational neglect and child maltreatment: the vast majority of people (about 80 percent) responsible for child maltreatment are the children's parents.[18]

SEXUAL ABUSE

Sexual abuse does not occur in a vacuum. It is most often accompanied by other forms of stress and trauma—generally within a family.[19]

Sexual abuse victims are three times more likely to suffer depression, six times more likely to experience post-traumatic stress disorder (PTSD), thirteen times more likely to abuse alcohol, and twenty-six times more likely to abuse drugs than those who have not been sexually abused.[20]

PTSD AND IMPACT OF TRAUMA

Veterans and their families deal with the painful aftermath of combat. Up to 20 percent of veterans and their families develop PTSD.[21] A report of child abuse is made every ten seconds in the United States.[22] Children who experience child abuse, and neglect are 59 percent more likely to be arrested as juveniles. These abused children are also 28 percent more likely to be arrested as an adult and 30 percent more likely to commit a violent crime.[23] On average, one person dies by suicide every 16.2 minutes. Each death intimately affects at least six other people.[24]

These statistics evidence how satan uses trauma as a tactical maneuver to wound, bruise, and paralyze believers and nonbelievers alike. Although the attack of trauma is widespread, there is hope and healing in God. The plan of God will always prevail over the plans and purposes of satan.

Demonic Squatters

We must not be "ignorant of [satan's] devices," "lest [satan] should take advantage of us" (2 Cor. 2:11 NKJV). We know the human body was created by God to house the spirit and the soul of man.

The body was designed as a physical dwelling place for the spirit of God to occupy the spirit of man for communion and fellowship.

Satan wants to use the body of a man as a habitation for his demonic spirits, which we call *demonic squatters*. A squatter is anyone who illegally occupies a property that they have no rights to reside in. A squatter remains in the property, refusing to leave, as if they own the property. Satan uses trauma to plant demonic squatters in the body, mind, and spirit of humans. Demonic squatters can manifest as anger, violence, murder, illness, disease, and the like.

> For this purpose the Son of God was manifested, that he might destroy the works of the devil. (1 John 3:8)

From the beginning, the devil has worked to corrupt God's creation.

STRONGHOLDS

After a specific experience or series of traumatic experiences, demonic squatters influence behaviors, attitudes, and perceptions and become strongholds (anything that holds on to you strongly outside of the counsel of God). These strongholds manifest as spirits of torment, fear, inadequacy, jealousy, suspicion, mistrust, guilt, suicide, shame, doubt, and perversion. Strongholds become stuck or lodged in the mind, body, spirit, and soul of a person as a result of trauma.

DYSFUNCTION

The impact of trauma can result in the cynical expectation of future abuse and become a self-fulfilling prophecy, leading to disabling beliefs and dysfunction of pathological behaviors. God is interested in bringing new life to our spirit and liberating us from dysfunction.

The Redemptive Work Continues

The redemptive work of Christ at Calvary did not remove all suffering from humanity. Until Christ returns, as a blood-washed sanctified believer you will be wounded, bruised, abused, betrayed, rejected, mocked, beaten, denied, lied about, and abandoned. When you give your life to Jesus Christ and become a believer, *your spirit is immediately redeemed.* Your *soul is being redeemed* through the renewing of your mind. *Your body will be redeemed* again when Jesus returns, and mortality takes on immortality.

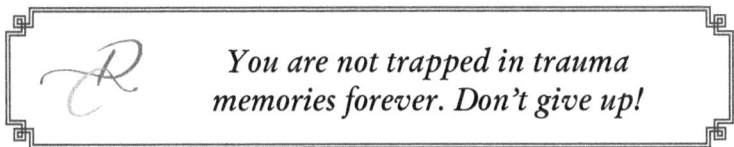

You are not trapped in trauma memories forever. Don't give up!

God desires to bring wholeness to our bodies. Our bodies are the vessels through which God's will is fulfilled. We have an eternal promise from God that one day both death and suffering will be no more (1 Cor. 15:54; Rom. 8:18; Rev. 21:4).

You Can Rewire Your Brain

Satan is not the only one with a plan. As the devil attempts to bring us into bondage, God offers a pathway to healing, deliverance, and recovery.

> Moreover, the God of all grace, who called you to his eternal glory in Christ, after you have suffered a while, will himself restore you and make you strong, firm and steadfast. (1 Peter 5:10)

You can rewire your brain. You can rebuild areas affected by trauma. You can take dominion over your life. Therefore, despite whatever has happened to you, it is not over yet. Jesus is Lord.

The Body Remembers

Renowned trauma expert Bessel van der Kolk, author of *The Body Keeps the Score*, says, "[Trauma] has to do with your body being reset to interpret the world as a dangerous place."[25]

That reset begins in the deep recesses of the brain's structural regions. These regions include areas dedicated to pleasure, engagement, control, and trust. The body keeps score, rearranges to the brain's wiring, and continues to remember the trauma. The body remembers what the mind wants to forget, and as van der Kolk says, no cognitive therapy can access it.

The good news is you can regain control of your body by rewiring your brain. You are not trapped in the effects and memories of trauma forever. Don't give up. Don't give in! Don't throw in the towel, because that is what the devil wants.

Chapter 1

Trauma, Memory, and the Vicissitudes of Life

A traumatic event can disrupt the body's natural equilibrium. A wealth of relevant research is documented in journals of medicine and psychology on the effects of trauma. A common denominator of the effect of trauma is that it is an unscheduled, out-of-ordinary life event, incredibly stressful and overwhelming, and may also challenge a person's core beliefs about which they are, their security and overall purpose in life.[1]

The vicissitudes of life in general have unscheduled events that can shape the human experiences and challenge one's beliefs about their ability to deal with threats to their psychological safety. The lenses in which we use to think, feel, assess threat, learn, remember, view the world, and make sense of things and those within the world are all profoundly altered by traumatic experiences."[2]

Two Storages of Memory

Traumatic memories are stored in many different parts of the brain, and the incident is remembered in two separate ways. Short term memory is stored in the hippocampus and serves as the first memory storages of the event itself and *replayed* as a cinematic video scene, but not under your will. The second memory consists entirely of the emotion, experienced in the *amygdala*, where negative feelings are triggered by what happened.[3]

THE TIMELESS AMYGDALA

According to neuroscientific research, traumatic memories can remain stuck in the amygdala. The amygdala affects the whole brain as it detects fear and stores and encodes negative memories into the hippocampus. (The hippocampus is located next to the amygdala and is essential for short-term memory in the amygdala and long-term memory storage in the cerebral cortex.) The amygdala is the part of the limbic system (referred to as the emotional brain) and is a set of brain structures that mediate intense emotions such as fear and anxiety.

There are no time-related distinctions made within the amygdala of when a disturbing event took place. In general, it takes around three hundred milliseconds for a person to become aware of an alarming incident. The amygdala reacts to the event within twenty seconds; the amygdala recalls what has happened but not when it happened.[4]

Fight or Flight Impulse

Without a point of reference to the timing of a past trauma event, a victim may experience a blind panic without any knowledge of a present threat. This panic triggers a "fight or flight" response (a physiological survival impulse reaction not under conscious control when a human or an animal feels threatened), experienced in the brain stem with communication to other parts of the limbic system (the emotional brain).[5]

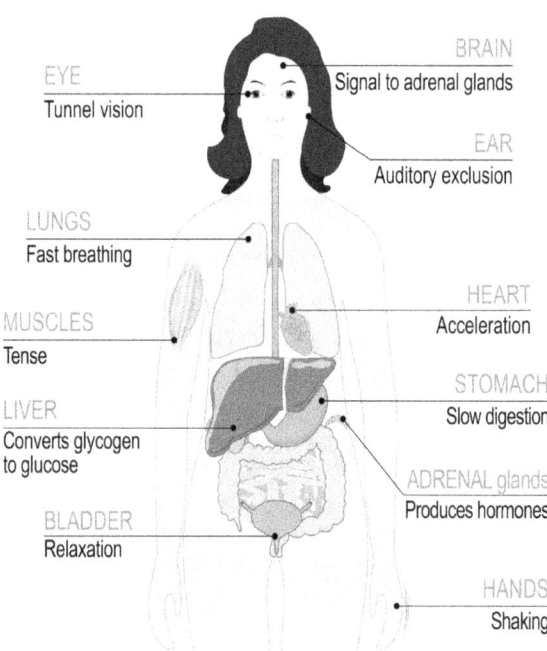

Figure 2

For instance, if someone who has experienced rape sees a person with similar features of the rapist approaching them, the victim's eyes may dilate, their heart may begin to palpitate, respiration increases, and they start to hyperventilate, freeze, or panic with fear. Even though the person is not in any immediate danger, intense emotions get wired faster than memories with little or no feelings.

Traumatization

When a person's emotional resources are inadequate to cope with an external threat, traumatization occurs. When a person witnesses, anticipates, or experiences an actual event or events, including the threat of death or serious injury or a threat to the physical integrity of one's self or others, the emotional trauma is encoded in the amygdala.[6]

The memory of the trauma creates stress in the hypothalamus, a part of the brain that is sensitive to stress and activates the release of cortisol, a stress-related hormone. The stress hormones tend to evoke two emotional extremes: 1) feeling too much emotion (overwhelmed) and 2) feeling too little emotion or feeling numb, whereby emotions are detached from thoughts, behaviors, and memories.[7]

When feeling too little emotions or during numbing response periods, one can become sensitive to traumatic stimuli that precipitate the hyper-arousal and emergency responses that may not be directly related to the original traumatic event but still causes intense reactions and become conditioned to elicit fear and anxiety.[8]

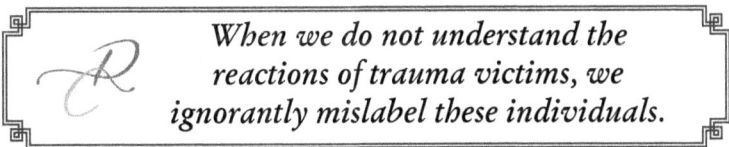

When we do not understand the reactions of trauma victims, we ignorantly mislabel these individuals.

HEIGHTENED AROUSAL RESPONSE

In response to an environmental stimulus, a trauma victim is prone to go immediately from stimulus to a heightened state of arousal without discerning what is actually going on in their environment. During a heightened state of arousal, a trauma victim, due to the deregulation of the body's brain chemistry resulting from a conditional stimuli response, may shut down, freeze, or overact to avoid stimuli reminiscent of the trauma. The alteration of brain chemistry can effect the brain for decades.[9]

Repeated Trauma

Many traumatized people expose themselves, seemingly compulsively, to situations reminiscent of the original trauma.[10] Trauma can be repeated on behavioral, emotional, physiological, and neuro-endocrinologic levels, exacerbated by exposure to continuing high levels of stress resulting in individual and social suffering.

"Anger directed against the self or others is always a central problem among those who have been violated, and this is itself a repetitive reenactment of real past events. . . . Anger begins in early childhood as a natural response to the failure of others to meet one's needs for love, praise, and acceptance."[11]

High-Risk Behaviors

Higher-than-expected risk populations, such as those who suffer from historical trauma, are more likely to engage in high-risk behaviors to cope with trauma. Historical trauma may motivate such behaviors as illegal activities, and substance use may serve as adaptive response patterns and modes of protection against powerful stimuli and the victim's attempt to cope with continuing psychological devastation.[12]

Mislabeling Maladaptive Behaviors

When we do not understand the reactions of trauma victims, we often judge them only by what we see. We don't seek to understand the underlying circumstances that birthed the responses and behaviors we now see.

Ignorantly, we mislabel these individuals as irrational, immoral, illogical, or crazy. We do not understand the fabric and traumatic thread which has been woven throughout their lives. We erroneously judge them with whatever limited knowledge (and prejudice) we have of how people should behave.

Trauma care requires understanding and compassion. We must understand the cycles created by trauma to liberate those entrapped in them. We can no longer dismiss traumatized persons due to their responses. We must pause to examine what has brought about certain behaviors we observe. Then we must recognize that the affected individual is trapped in a cycle and encourage them to pursue deliverance from clergy or a practitioner who can facilitate the stages of deliverance, healing, and recovery.

Trauma, Memory, and the Vicissitudes of Life

CHAPTER 2

Algorithms, Codes, and Data Files

The human brain can be compared to a computer. Four components comprise a computer: the memory or storage device, the processor unit (CPU) or hardware, and the input and output devices. Each component performs and processes specialized task functions independently through a series of coded algorithms that are stored in memory and retrieved as data output. Computers use both hardware and software to handle data similar to our brain according to a set of instructions that travel through electrical circuits.

The software gives commands to the hardware so the computer will function. Similarly, the mind is the signaler, and the brain is the receiver. The CPU is the brain of the machine and responsible for interpreting every code input by users or from external sensors it receives from the other computer components and making it usable to the operating system.[1]

The Body's Command Center

The human brain is a three-pound organ, yet just another organ the Holy Spirit resides in. Understanding how the nervous system develops, including the structure of the brain and what it does, is a science referred to as *neuroscience*. The study of neuroscience is complex, and scientists are still trying to unravel some of the unknown mysteries of brain operations. What we do know is that the brain interprets information from the outside world, controls all function of the body, is protected by a skull, and embodies the essence of the mind and soul.[2]

CEREBRUM

The brain has three primary layers (God seems to create in threes) which control body functions: the forebrain, or *cerebrum*; the midbrain, or *cerebellum*; and the hindbrain, or *brain stem*.

The cerebrum is the most substantial part of the brain and the uppermost region of the central nervous system. The cerebrum is divided into two halves: the right and left hemispheres. These two hemispheres are joined together by a bundle of fibers (called the corpus callosum) that transmits messages between the regions.[3]

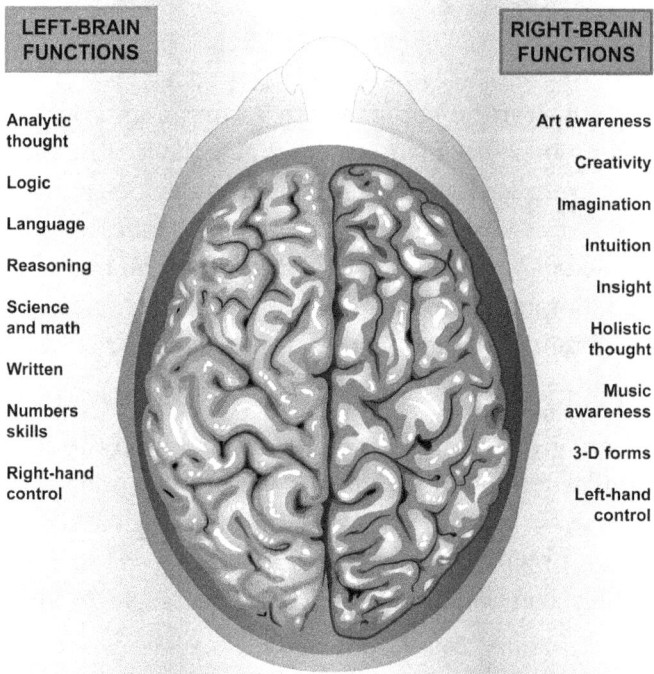

Figure 3: The cerebrum

RIGHT AND LEFT HEMISPHERES

The right hemisphere is associated with emotional states, including intuition, creativity, autonomic arousal, and holding images and themes. It stores memories as pictures in the brain, but just talking about the pictures embedded does not remove them.

The left side of the brain does all the thinking including the motivation to apply logical reasoning and meaning to our thought processes and adding words to feelings and perceptions. The left brain is involved in regulation and awareness of conscious emotions. Each hemisphere controls the opposite side of the body.

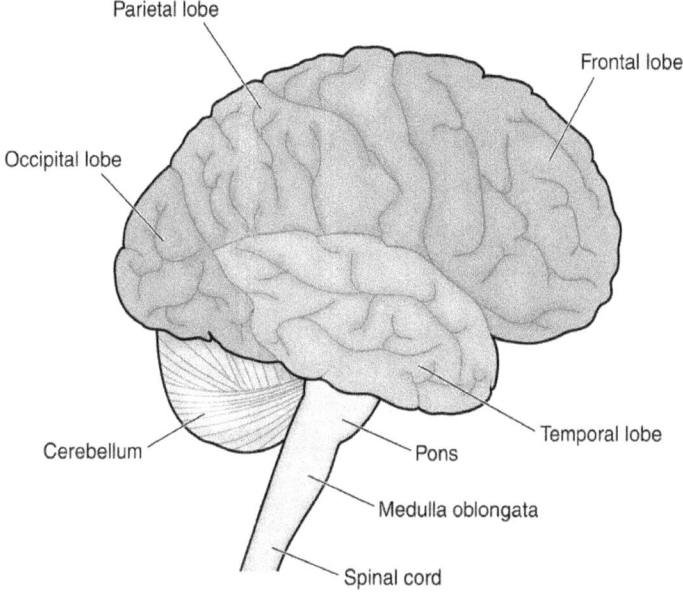

Figure 4: Four Lobes of the Cerebrum

The cerebrum regulates all other parts of the brain and is divided into four lobes: the frontal lobe, parietal lobe, occipital lobe, and temporal lobe. The *prefrontal cortex* (PFC) is the cerebral cortex covering the front part of the frontal lobe and is the most advanced region of the brain. It is the CEO or supervisory system of the integration of emotional and cognitive function and controls voluntary movements. The *parietal lobe* processes information about temperature, taste, touch, and movement. The *occipital lobe* is primarily responsible for vision. The *temporal lobe* is responsible for a range of functions including reasoning and auditory perception.[4]

The limbic system is another portion of the cerebrum and is associated with the emotions. It is responsible for emotional regulation, planning, managing uncertainty, reappraisal, changes in perceptions, interpreting touch, vision, hearing, and speech, error detection, belief and behaviors, reasoning, emotions, control of movement, learning, self-reflection, and inferences about others' morality.[5]

In summary, three major components of the brain (limbic system, brain stem, and cerebral cortex) control body functions, movement, thought, and behaviors and can make a difference in how we think, feel, and respond to fear, threat, and anxiety. Our emotional reaction and response to life can be triggered easily by trauma experiences and can control our behavior and emotional response to environmental triggers without our awareness.

THE LIMBIC SYSTEM (EMOTIONAL BRAIN)

The limbic system is a set of brain structures (hypothalamus, hippocampus, and amygdala) in the limbic system that lays deep inside the brain on both sides of the thalamus, immediately beneath the cerebrum.[6]

The limbic system generates emotional information on an unconsciousness level via signals (data in) from our thoughts and the five senses (sound, sight, touch, taste, and smell) then sends the information to the frontal lobes for conscious interpretation. "The frontal lobes mediate the emotional intensity (data output) and work in tandem with the limbic system to influence our experience and the response to the experience and processes feelings of pleasure, such as those experienced from eating and sex; and feelings of survival, such as fear and anger."[7]

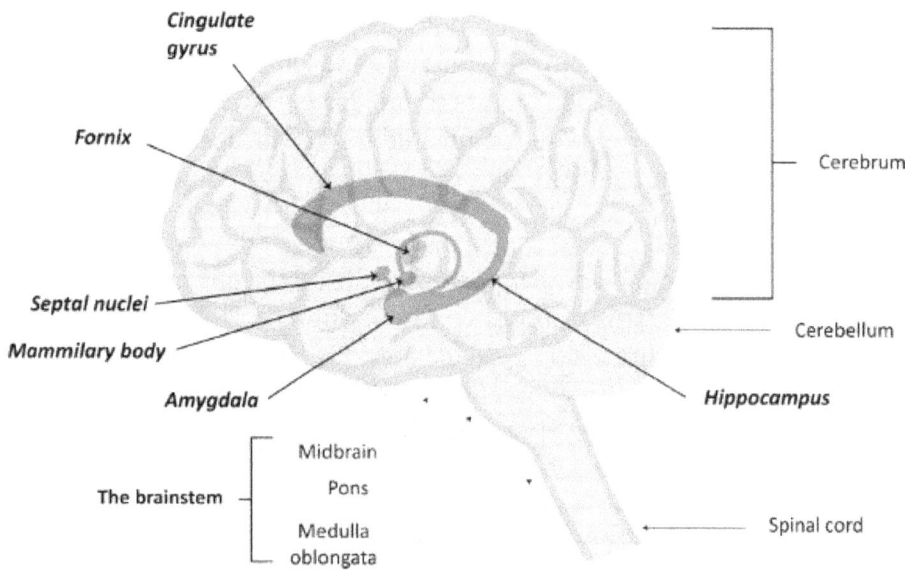

Figure 5: The Limbic System

The limbic system is not a separate system but a collection of structures and interlinking parts whose function is to control aspects related to the preservation of oneself and survival of the human species. Parts of the limbic system includes the amygdala, hypothalamus, hippocampus, basal ganglia, and cingulate gyrus.[8]

Amygdala

The amygdala is considered the alarm circuit of the brain; it detects and responds to danger and helps ensure our survival in the presence of harmful threats. The amygdala mediates emotions such as fear, threat, and anxiety; it is located below the neocortex (the outer covering of the brain) that underlies thinking, planning and even consciousness. The amygdala can encode negative memories into the hippocampus, which is responsible for short-term memory. Both structures can activate the other consciously or unconsciously.[9]

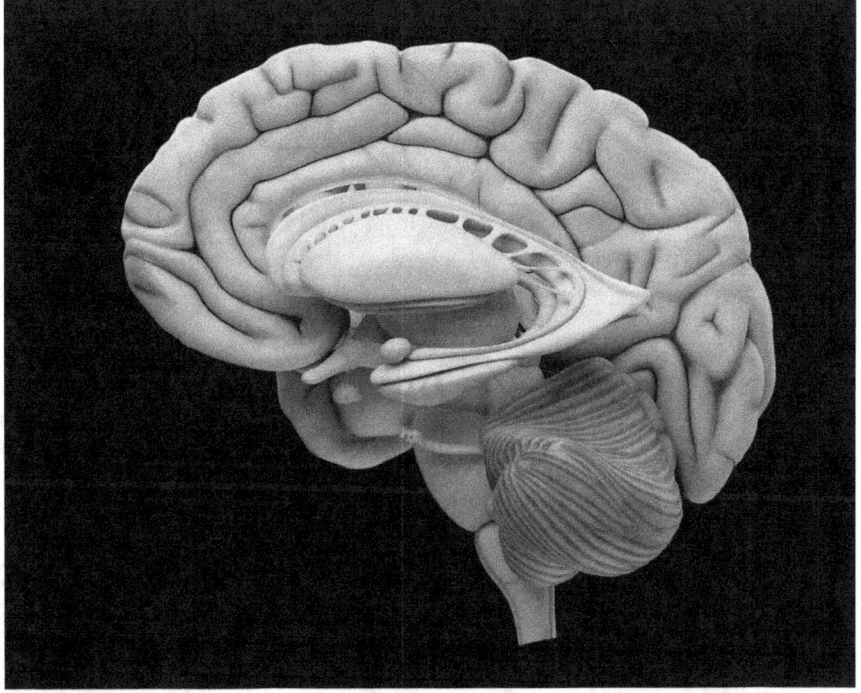

Figure 6: Amygdala

Hypothalamus

The hypothalamus is a subcortical component of the limbic system and receives incoming information through our senses: sight, smell, hearing, touch, and taste. Information is then passed on to other parts of the brain for processing. The thalamus relays sensory information to the amygdala, which stamps and embeds traumatic events as emotionally significant and simultaneously stores it for future use to avoid related threats. It plays an essential role in the formation of new memories, encoding new information, converting short-term memory into lasting, long-term memories, and processing past experiences, facts, feelings, thoughts.[10]

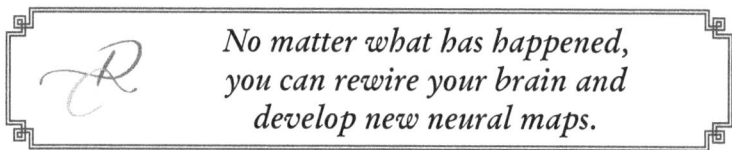

No matter what has happened, you can rewire your brain and develop new neural maps.

Hippocampus

The hippocampus is primarily associated with short-term memory and encoding new information and the storage of long-term memories. It is also responsible for the memory of the location of objects or people.

The hippocampus is located next to the amygdala. It provides contextual meaning to stimuli and controls our emotional response by transforming sensory stimuli into emotional and hormonal signals, then refers this information to other parts of the brain that control behavior. The hippocampus is sensitive to stress hormones, which control one's mood, motivation, and fear. Without a functional hippocampus, normal memory retention is not possible.[11]

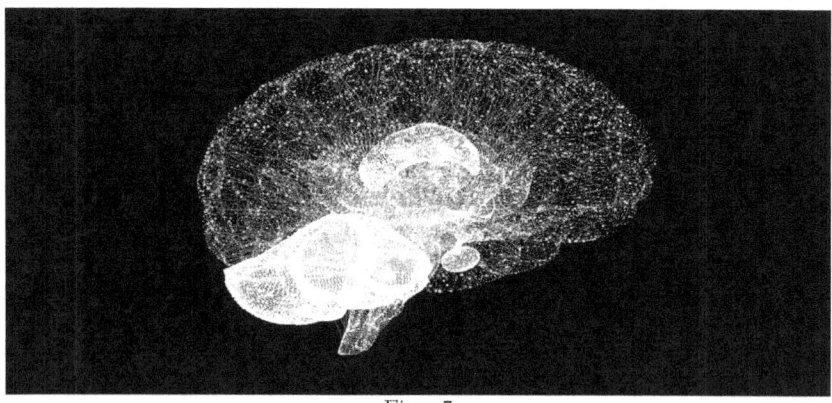

Figure 7

Basal Ganglia

The basal ganglia receive extensive input from the cerebral cortex and thalamus. They are responsible for the formation of behavioral habits, which are crucial for energy efficiency for the brain, coordinated movement including eye movement, and procedural learning including cognitive and emotional functions.[12]

CINGULATE GYRUS

The cingulate gyrus is the structure involved with the detection of errors, accessing risk-based decisions, conflict management, response inhibition, cognitive control, adaptation, and autonomic motor function and behavior regulation. Often referred to as the "accountant" of the brain, it accesses risk-based decision and determines if an action corresponds with one's belief systems.[13] Messages can travel from one gyrus (a ridge on the cerebral cortex) to another, from one lobe to another, from one side of the brain to the other, and other structures deep in the brain.[14]

CEREBELLUM

The cerebellum, or the hindbrain, is the second most significant part of the brain. It is located under the cerebrum behind the top part of the brain stem (where the spinal cord meets the brain). The cerebellum is made of two hemispheres (halves). Its primary function involves coordinating motor movement, balance, equilibrium, and information from the sensory systems and other parts of the brain and contributes in the basic memory storage and motor responses of the brain.[15]

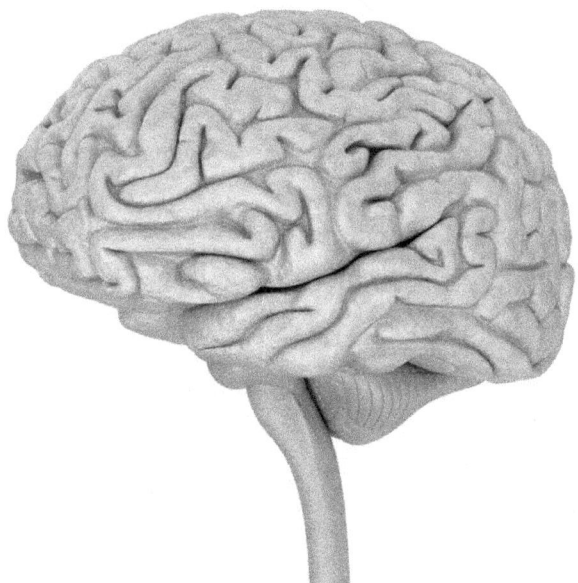

Figure 8: Cerebellum and brain stem

Brainstem

The brainstem acts as a relay center connecting the cerebrum and cerebellum to the spinal cord. It is reactive to emotional triggers of fear, threat, and anxiety, real or imaginative, on an unconscious level. The brain stem is also responsible for our most primitive instinctive behaviors (flight, fright, fight) and serves essential functions in motor movement, movements of the eye, and auditory and visual processing.[16] It is involved in essential life-support functions and performs many automatic, unconscious bodily functions, such as breathing, heart rate, and regulating the flow of energy through different parts of the body.

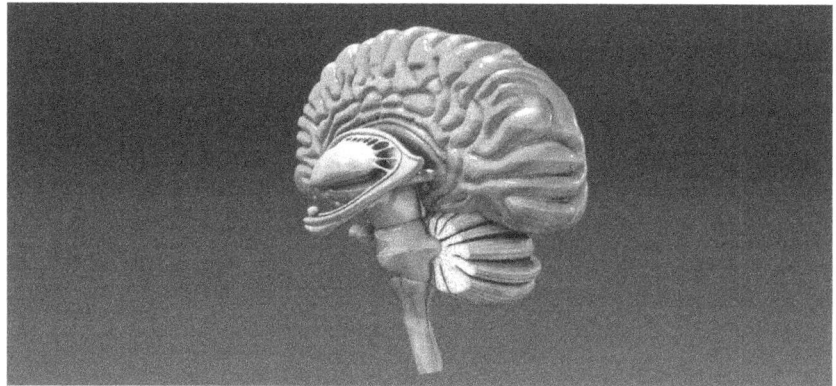

Figure 9: The Brainstem

How Does the Brain Work?

As human beings, we think and learn through a series of neural connections or pathways. The brain receives information through our five senses: sight, smell, touch, taste, and hearing, sometimes simultaneously. It assembles the messages in a way that has meaning for us and stores that information in our memory.[17]

Images are perceived through a series of biochemical, electrical impulses sent out by the senses. This perception comes after the left and right side of the brain process and decodes the images for sense-making. Specialized organs and tissues exert centralized control through electrochemical events via two major divisions: the peripheral nervous system (PNS) and the central nervous system (CNS).[18]

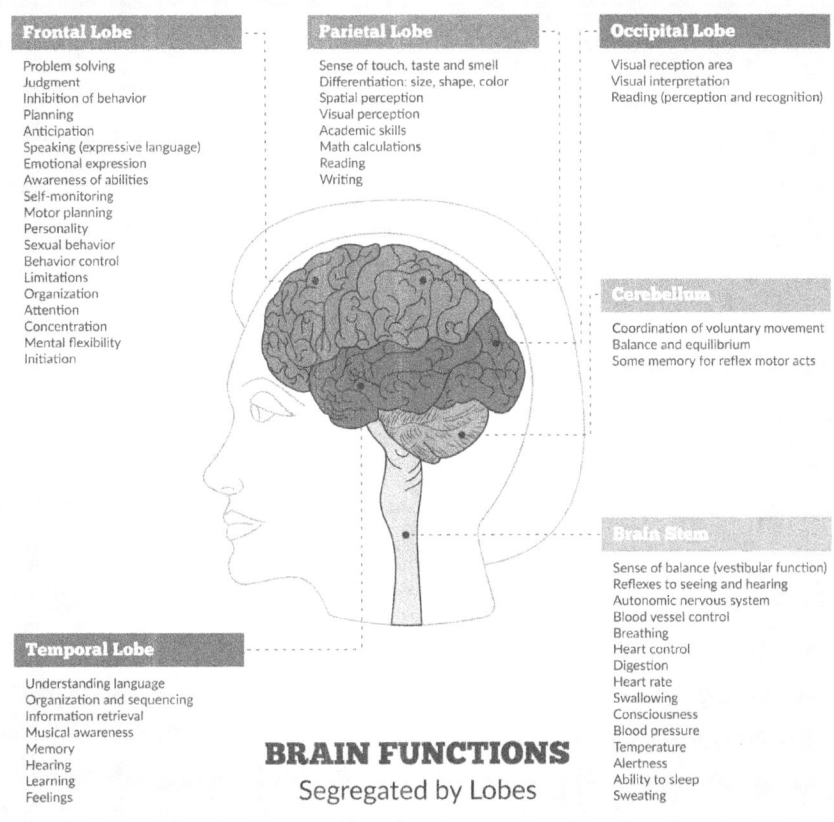

Figure 10

GRAY AND WHITE MATTER

The brain is divided into two categories: gray matter and white matter. Gray matter, making up about 40 percent of the brain and found in all parts of the brain, takes up 94 percent of the brain's oxygen. The gray matter serves to process information generated in sensory organs. The male brain utilizes nearly *seven times more* gray matter for activity than the female brain.

White matter makes up the other 60 percent of the brain. *Female brains* utilize nearly *ten times more* white matter. The primary function of white matter is to regulate the electrical signals in axons. These signals are a form of communication and work to pass along information which translates into chemical signals between neurons.[19]

Nerve and Glial Cells

The brain is made up of two types of cells: nerve cells (neurons) and glial cells. Neurons are information-processing cells that receive, integrate, and transmit information through the nervous system of the body.[20] Glial cells surround the neurons and provide support for and insulation between them.[21] Though neural networks are comprised of eighty-six billion connected neurons, the brain defines a recognizable linear pathway.

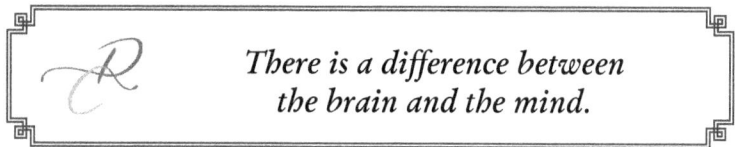

There is a difference between the brain and the mind.

The Mind Shapes the Brain

There is a difference between the brain and the mind. The brain is made of physical matter and is the place where the mind resides. It is a vessel God uses to communicate on a conscious level with man and where electronic impulses that create thought are contained.

The mind shapes the brain; it is the limitless source that regulates the flow of energy in the brain.[22] For instance, if you constantly worry and engage in negative thoughts, such as self-condemnation, anger, and criticism, then your brain will gradually take that shape. The brain will develop neural structures and dynamics of anxiety, low sense of worth, and a similar projection to others. On the other hand, if you regularly set your mind upon seeing the good in self and others, then the brain will gradually take the shape of strength, self-confidence, and inner peace.[23]

> "Finally, brethren, whatsoever things are true, whatsoever things are honest, whatsoever things are just, whatsoever things are pure, whatsoever things are lovely, whatsoever things are of good report; if there be any virtue, and if there be any praise, think on these things." (Phil. 4:8)

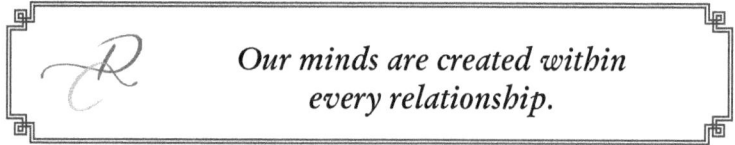

Our minds are created within every relationship.

NEURAL NETWORKS

As I mentioned earlier, images are perceived through a series of biochemical, electrical impulses which form a neuro-network that's sent out by the senses after the left and right side of the brain process and decode the images for sense-making.[24]

RELATIONSHIPS CREATE THE MIND

Created within our mind is the relationship between others and with one's self. We are individually and uniquely made with a divine purpose and destiny. No two people have the same fingerprint or mind. Our thoughts, feelings, perceptions, memories, beliefs, and attitudes have a specific pattern shaped by culture and experience. These patterns shape the flow of energy and information inside us, and we share them with other minds.[25]

NEUROPLASTICITY

Whatever you experience or imagine physically changes the brain. This is called *experience-dependent neuroplasticity*.[26] Neuroplasticity enables the brain to create new neural circuitry throughout life.[27]

REMEMBERING CHANGES MEMORY

Scientists have recently learned that the very act of remembering changes the memory itself. Every memory begins as a changed set of connections among trillions of cells (neurons) that act in conjunction with one another and are stored in different ways and in different parts of the brain. The brain "replays" a pattern of neural activity that was initially generated in response to a particular event.

New information suggests that memories are not concrete or frozen in time but rather are a mirror of the brain's perception of the actual event and may become incorporated into old memories over time.[28]

IMPLICIT MEMORIES

As we've learned in chapter 1, trauma events and related memories become encoded directly in the brain as implicit memories. These memories are deeply imprinted by the amygdala. Furthermore, they are imprinted deeper than everyday recollections and may manifest as feelings of anger, rage, sadness, mistrust, fear, shame, loneliness, and abandonment.[29]

Author's Note

Trauma healing and treatment involves processing trauma-related memories. There are multiple pathways to storage of fear-inducing memories, which cause the memory to be stored differently.[30]

The body seeks to maintain an equilibrium and homeostasis within the conscious mind and tries to make sense of things that are often senseless. The individual's existing mental schema or mental map (sense-making process) may be entirely unable to integrate a specific terrifying experience and therefore might not be available for the act of remembering. Memories that do not pose a threat or form a contradiction to our existing mental schema, beliefs, values, and meanings of the world may be integrated in the subconscious.[31]

Each of us sees the world from a glass dimly lit and integrates our present worldview with our past experiences, behaviors, and future expectations using looking-glass self-perspective, based on how one believes others perceive them.

These experiences are etched in our memories like data on a computer chip. The memories are stored, backed up, and retrievable no matter how forgetful we may think we are.

The trauma experience in the following narrative provides an example of how the brain stores memory.

Case #1 Trauma Narrative

Charlotte is a forty-three-year-old divorced former New York City police officer. She is the mother of a twelve-year-old. Charlotte accepted Christ at the age of thirty-five and is now an ordained minister of the gospel.

Charlotte is of Caribbean heritage. She grew up in the South Bronx with two dysfunctional parents. Her father was an alcoholic, and her mother had a mental illness. Her father was a roofer who seldom worked; instead, he used her mother's welfare check to buy himself liquor.

Charlotte's father was born and raised in North Carolina. He had very little education, having reached only the sixth grade. He grew up in an impoverished household by parents who were both alcoholics.

For most of Charlotte's childhood, she watched her father drink and never live a productive life. Charlotte's father followed a predictable pattern. He left the house sober at around six in the morning and returned home hours later intoxicated. He slept until the alcohol wore off, before going out to drink some more.

Charlotte preferred it when her father was drunk because he was not as mean and belligerent as he was when sober. Whether drunk or sober, he was not loving or affectionate. He often told Charlotte she was ugly and stupid.

In describing the impact of this verbal trauma, Charlotte says, "The fear I had of him I still carry today; however, God is delivering me from the spirit of fear."

Although Charlotte's mother had a mental illness, she was a loving parent. "I remember her cooking at times and taking us to the store," Charlotte says fondly. "When she received her welfare check, she kept me home from school, and we would go shopping."

Charlotte's mother's mental illness did affect the family. Charlotte felt embarrassed by her mother's illness when out in their neighborhood because her mother talked to herself and always spoke loudly.

Charlotte's father did not know how to deal with her mother's illness. He beat her mother at times. Charlotte saw her father hit her mother in the face and throw her down to the floor. He also pimped her mother out to men every week, and Charlotte witnessed some of these sexual encounters. She said her mother did not seem to resist.

"Did she even realize what her husband was doing to her was wrong?" Charlotte wondered in sessions.

One morning when Charlotte was around six or eight years old, her mother took her to the doctor; she told the doctor she wanted to know who had raped her daughter. The doctor asked Charlotte many questions. The police came and asked Charlotte who had raped her.

Charlotte said, "I never knew what prompted her to take me to the doctor or even thinking that I had been raped. If I was raped, I could not remember. I remember that I was at the doctor's office to be treated for a sexually transmitted disease called gonorrhea."

Charlotte stated that her memory of her childhood and of her siblings is fragmented. She grew up never remembering who the rapist was until one day the Holy Spirit revealed it to her in a dream. Upon waking abruptly, she realized it was her father who had raped her as a child.

With her heart racing in disbelief, Charlotte remembers saying to herself, "I never thought a father could do such a heinous thing to a child." She thanked the Holy Spirit for revealing this to her. Today she still has no recollection of the rape itself but believes she suffers from the effects.

At the age of twenty-one, she married a man who was emotionally abusive. He only married her to get US citizenship. Charlotte has said, "The only bright spot in that marriage was the birth of my daughter." Her ex-husband rejected her, much like her father did. This left Charlotte's self-esteem shattered for many years. Charlotte is now in the process of rebuilding her self-esteem through counseling and by studying the Word of God.

Charlotte has been in counseling off and on for more than thirty years, trying to repair the damage created by the traumatic event she experienced. In an attempt to avoid the painful memories of her childhood, she would sit in a chair, rock back and forth, and daydream for hours at a time. This daydreaming allowed her to mentally ignore the things that had taken place in her life. The daydreams gave her an escape from the thoughts that come from being part of a dysfunctional family.

This maladaptive dreaming started during her childhood and continued into her adult life. Maladaptive daydreaming is a condition that causes intense daydreaming and serves to distract an individual from their real life. It is something Charlotte still struggles with but less so since she accepted the call into ministry at the age of thirty-four. The maladaptive daydreaming has been debilitating to her in many ways. She has lost time and opportunities she could have pursued had she not been daydreaming. For many years it kept her isolated at home. Her college studies, family, and employment as a police officer have also suffered. Charlotte was forced into retirement because of it.

Her daydreams were filled with characters. She created characters and made up stories about them. If she could not become the person she desired to be, then she would create that person in her imagination. The characters created in her mind were never abused. They lived a beautiful and fulfilling life. In her daydreams, she created two abandoned sisters who were found as children by a kind man who sent them both to college in Australia. One sister became a doctor and the other, a teacher.

The sisters would talk to each other, and Charlotte would sometimes get lost all day in their intimate conversations. The men in the sisters' lives were respectful, loving, and honest—the opposite of what Charlotte has experienced in her real-life relationships. Her prayer is that the dream of being in a healthy relationship with a man would one day become a reality. She acknowledges that she is not dating.

Suggested Approach and Prayer Focus:

I would encourage Charlotte and anyone else who has experienced a similar trauma to discover and know they can experience wholeness by embracing the prayer declarations in Appendix 4 (at the back of this book). When paired with the strategy to rewire your brain (outlined in chapter 11), you can begin the initial steps toward trauma-wound healing and deliverance designed to promote recovery.

Algorithms, Codes, and Data Files

CHAPTER 3

Taxonomies of Traumas

Experiencing trauma can impact a person's neurological functioning. A plethora of research exists on the effects of chronic stress on physical, psychological, familial, and social functioning and suggests that each person has a degree of vulnerability or threshold.[1]

Trauma causes physiological changes in the central and peripheral nervous system that regulate whole physiological interactions and body functioning.[2]

Triggers and Automatic Responses

After a traumatic event, the amygdala responds to stimuli within thirty seconds—before any evaluation of the stimuli or time frame. Many people have an overactive amygdala and remain on constant alert for trauma reminders and may be the reason for a person re-experiencing the event due to the traumatic reminder, which often results in hyperactivation. The hyperactivation of the amygdala "may be responsible for symptoms of hyperarousal in PTSD, including exaggerated startle responses, irritability, anger outbursts, and general hypervigilance."[3]

Perceived Threats after Trauma

After the original trauma takes place, an external reminder of the initial trauma like a sound, face, smell, or gesture will cause the body to automatically respond to the perceived threat, without a person consciously being aware of the response. Research reveals that "emotionally arousing stimuli are more strongly remembered than emotionally neutral stimuli." The amygdala gives emotional meaning to the external stimuli; however, the hippocampus provides contextual meaning to the stimuli.[4]

Figure :11 Trauma Tree

Value Processors

Human beings are purported to be value processors, meaning we develop a type of an internal self-appraisal system comprise of a person's beliefs, preconceptions, interpretation, and attitudes. This system shapes how we process and cope with out-of-ordinary trauma events.[5]

Trauma Taxonomies

Traumas are differentiated by two classifications and the type of traumatic event. The first classification is based on individual internal function. The second classification is based on passed-down traumas (external) to an individual.[6]

Internal Traumas

The first taxonomy is based on the individual (internal) function. Five traumatic event types are included as internal traumas: attachment trauma, autonomy (or identity) trauma, interdependence trauma, achievement (or self-actualization trauma), and survival trauma.

Attachment Trauma

Attachment trauma occurs when a child's feelings of attachment or companionship with an adult are off balance or rejected. Typical examples include divorce or death of a parent.

Autonomy Trauma

Autonomy or identity trauma is trauma that damages a person's self-efficacy or sense of identity. This type of trauma may include sexual assault or domestic violence.

Interdependence Trauma

Interdependence trauma occurs when an individual's social network or support system is threatened. This compromises feelings of safety and security.

Achievement or Self-Actualization Trauma

Achievement or self-actualization trauma may include the failure to "achieve a target that is perceived as essential to survival or progression. . . . Examples of self-actualization trauma are lay-off, demotion, and substantial loss of money, health, or valuables, substantial failures to achieve life goals."[7]

Survival Trauma

Survival trauma occurs when a person experiences an event in which they believed their life was in danger. Examples of such trauma include surviving a terminal illness, natural disaster, military combat, or traffic accidents.

Factitious Trauma

The second taxonomy classification is based on external criteria and includes two main categories: trauma-like or factitious and real traumatic events. The internal trauma may be secondary, meaning that the trauma is not experienced by the person but rather by a loved one and then transmitted to the person.[8]

One-Step Transmission of Trauma

One-step transmission of trauma occurs when a loved one encounters the traumatic event, but the person who is indirectly involved is still affected. Parents may experience one-step transmission of secondary trauma if their child is a victim of sexual assault.[9] Here we can see how the transmission of spirit can be transferred from one individual to another, including the transmission by the laying on of hands.

Intergenerational Transmission of Trauma

Traumas can be transmitted cross-generationally passed down from generation to generation in self-perpetuating cycles that are hard to break. Cross generationally trauma can be transmitted by two means: through the family or collectively in a group transmission. Cross-generationally is what is happening when vicious cycles of violence, physical abuse, or incest in a family occur generation after generation.[10]

Multi-generational Historical Trauma

The second kind of group trauma is the multi-generational transmission of structural violence characterized by extreme social disparities across generations. Historical trauma includes three successive phases:

The *first phase* entails the dominant culture perpetrating mass traumas on a population. The result is cultural, familial, societal and economic devastation such, unemployment, inadequate housing, low socioeconomic status, and malnutrition can all affect populations and multiple generations. This effect can lead to the chronic cycle of poverty and leave numerous generations at a disadvantage.

The *second phase* occurs when the original generation of the population responds to the trauma showing biological, societal, and psychological symptoms.

The *third phase* is when the initial responses to trauma are conveyed to successive generations through environmental and psychological factors and prejudice and discrimination.[11]

Historical Trauma

Native American social worker and mental health expert Maria Yellow Horse Brave Heart initially conceptualized the phrase *historical trauma* in the 1980s. Brave Heart defines historical trauma as "cumulative emotional and psychological wounding, over the lifespan and across generations, emanating from massive group trauma."[12]

Building on Brave Heart's scholarship and the research of other pioneers in this area, the technical definition of collective or historical trauma is "a blow to the underlying tissue of social life that happens to a large group of peoples and damages the bonds attaching people and impairs the prevailing sense of community."[13]

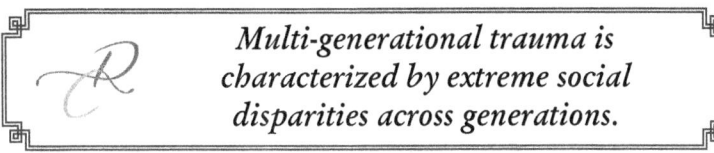

Multi-generational trauma is characterized by extreme social disparities across generations.

Modern Examples of Historical Trauma

Historical trauma, according to the compiled research, can result from colonialism, war, genocide, slavery, incarceration, terrorism, displacement, poverty, natural or human-made disasters, and more.[14] Not discounting the trauma of Native Americans, Jewish people, or any other oppressed group, the trauma of slavery and vestiges of racism still resonate today both on an individual and structural level, resulting in deep trauma wounds and bruises.

The surge of racial and bias attacks against people of color triggers a collective memory of slavery and still resonates among the descendants of enslaved Africans. Racial bias has a profound effect on the social, mental, and physical functioning of African Americans and other oppressed groups, impacting both the interaction with one another and their social environments.

Slave Narratives: Confession, Inhibition, and Resiliency Implications for Prevention and Policy

"Historical trauma" was the basis of investigation for my doctoral dissertation "Slave Narratives: Confession, Inhibition, and Resiliency Implications for Prevention and Policy."

The historical research study included the examination of over 230 slave narratives collected during the Great Depression by the Federal Writers' Project (FWP), the average age of the former slaves being eighty-five years old—and among whom nearly one in every ten claimed to be one hundred years old at the time of the interview.[15]

The slave narratives were used as sources to gain an understanding of the impact of the social experience of slavery on the former slaves and their health outcomes and to gain insight on how diverse causal paths of resilience become differentiated over time. I sought to understand differences in longevity between black and white people.

Recent studies have shown that the ethnic minorities of the United States have higher rates of morbidity and mortality as compared to their non-minorities counterpart. *Morbidity* refers to the state of being diseased or unhealthy within a population. *Mortality* is the term used for the number of people who died within a population. The life expectancy in the twenty-first century at birth for black males is 69.5 years, compared with 75.7 years for white males. For black females, life expectancy is 76.3 years, compared with 80.8 years for white females.[16] Mortality data based on the 1850 U.S. Bureau of the Census reveals there were more centenarians among blacks than whites in 1850 within the certain southern states.[17]

The research analyses of the population sample of over 230 slave narratives and other source data revealed that health disparities circumscribed the lives of former slaves. Their resiliency and mortality rate changed over time as their circumstances and situations changed. Moreover, the findings revealed the changes in their resiliency appeared to be explained by the timing of the influences of social inequalities. As disparities and racism changed, the resilient pathways (coping mechanisms, which once served to insulate former slaves from the effects of racism) left the former slaves more vulnerable to the consequences of poor health outcomes.

The 2002 Institute of Medicine (IOM) report defined disparities in health care as "racial or ethnic differences in the quality of health care that are not due to access-related factors or clinical needs, preferences, and appropriateness of intervention.[18]

In the more than one hundred forty years since the passing of the Thirteenth Amendment that officially eradicated slavery along with instinctive or unintentional servitude, little has changed about the impact of racism and prejudice on health disparities.[19] The Thirteenth Amendment concentrated on abolishing slavery and involuntary servitude; however, it did not eliminate racism and the discrimination of African Americans. Discrimination and racism are both still present in varied forms.

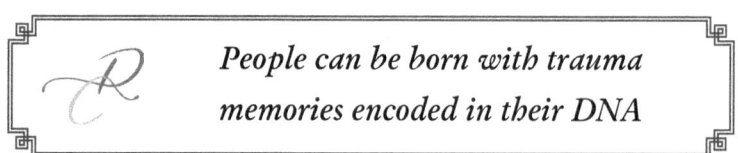

People can be born with trauma memories encoded in their DNA

The trauma experience in the following narrative is an example of how trauma can be transmitted cross-generationally. An individual may have witnessed domestic violence as a child and then seek relationships with partners who are abusive. This trauma can then be transmitted to the children of these parents, resulting in generational family trauma transmission.

Characters, ministries, or locations described in the narrative are fictitious, and any persons known to the reader is purely coincidental.

Case #2 Trauma Narrative

Paul is a single, unemployed, forty-six-year-old black man. Paul has a history of witnessing intimate partner violence between his mother and father. Paul's father was an alcoholic and was abusive to Paul and his mother. Paul blames his mother for accepting the abuse and repeatedly allowing his father to take out his anger out on them.

Paul lived with his parents as an only child until he was five years old, at which time Paul's half-brother, John, came to live with them after his release from jail. (John was twenty-six years old. He was born from a previous relationship Paul's father was in).

For several years, John sexually abused Paul. Paul remembers his brother saying, "This is our special way of becoming whole brothers instead of half- brothers." On one occasion during an act of sexual abuse, Paul's mother walked into the room and saw John on top of Paul with his pants down. Paul's mother began to scream at John and yelled for him to get off her son. She threatened John that she would tell his father and have him arrested.

As soon as his father came home that day, Paul's mother told him what she witnessed. His dad had been drinking as usual. Within moments, Paul's father went into a rage, yelling at his mother, "Stop lying, bitch."

"I want John out of this house," she told Paul's father. "I will call the police if you do not." Before she could finish her statement, Paul's father punched her in the mouth. Paul tried to intervene, but his father hit him in the chest, knocking him to the floor.

Paul begged his father to stop beating his mother, but he just kept beating and kicking her savagely. By this point, she was bleeding from her head, mouth, and nose. Paul thought if he could tell his father, reasoned to himself, *If I say John and I were wrestling and deny the abuse, he will stop hitting Mom.*

However, nothing would stop Paul's father. He accused Paul of being a "punk" and a liar just like his mother. The sexual abuse and domestic violence continued until Paul was twelve years old. Paul says the memory of that day still plays in his mind like a video with the volume on high.

Paul remembers nights when his father never came home. He liked those nights because when his father did come home, "he was abusive and would force my mother to have sex with him. Both my mother and I were living in prison." Paul once even heard his mother tell his father, "I should have never married you."

One morning when his father left to go to work, Paul's mother packed their clothes. They left for a week and stayed at his aunt's house. During their stay, his mother secured an order of protection. Paul recalls his mother waving the order of protection in his father's face, laughing under his breath.

His parents argued a bit that day, but then his father left. Paul never saw him again.

About a month later, Paul learned that his father died in a car accident. Paul did not go to the funeral. He hated his father and was glad he was dead. The day of the funeral, the police showed up at Paul's home. To his surprise, his mother had called the police after his father's death to report the years of abuse he had endured.

The police asked Paul what happened, and he told them that John had been sexually abusing him since he was six years old. When the police questioned his mother as to why she waited so long to report the crime, she said, "I was terrified that my husband would kill both of us."

John was still living with them at the time. John was dressed to go to the funeral when the police arrived. They arrested him on the spot and took him to jail. Paul had to undergo a physical examination for the investigation, and the findings would be used in court. The doctor testified that his investigation confirmed Paul's sexual abuse allegation. John was found guilty of rape and sentenced to fifteen years in prison.

At the age of twenty-one, Paul joined the Army ROTC program and obtained a bachelor's degree in computer technology. During his time in the Army, Paul had a few brushes with the law for drunken disorderly conduct and sexual harassment. As a result, he received a dishonorable discharge.

Over the years, Paul had difficulty maintaining employment and relationships. Eventually, he became self-employed and opened a geek store out of the house he lived in with his mother.

Throughout Paul's adult life, he dated several women. The longest relationship Paul has had is with Diane. They attend Grace Church of Deliverance (fictitious name) together. Paul serves as a member of the trustee board; Diane sings in the choir. Although they are active in their church, Paul often spends the night with her. Diane had mentioned marriage before, but in the past, Paul would make love to Diane, assuring that he was hers. This would suffice Diane for the time, and she would stop pressuring him to get married. One evening Paul went to Diane's apartment for dinner, as he often would. Paul had been drinking during dinner. Diane reminded Paul while at the table of their third anniversary.

"I want to get married for Christmas. I cannot just keep living in sin with you, Paul," Diane pleaded. Paul responded by telling her they did not need to get married. For some reason, Paul's typical plan did not work this time. Diane rejected all his advances. To force him to stop, Diane hit Paul over the head with a blunt object, causing blood to run down his head.

Afterward, Paul called his mother. She informed Paul that Diane had already called her saying she planned to get an order of protection against him for attempted rape. Paul told his mother that Diane was angry because he did not want to get married. As Paul shared the events surrounding the encounter, he said, "Would you believe that whore threatened to call the police if I didn't leave?" He later admitted that he might have been too sexually aggressive that night. He told his mother he was afraid the police would arrest him. Paul refused to take any responsibility for the situation. Paul's mother told him to give it some time.

She told Paul that Diane filing an order of protection didn't mean she didn't love him. Paul's mother said she filed three orders of protection against his father and later withdrew them.

Paul's mother pleaded with him to talk with his pastor. She urged Paul to ask God for forgiveness and deliverance from alcoholism, mainly since he was a deacon in the church. Paul told her that he and Diane had gone to the pastor. The pastor prayed with them and encouraged them to repent for living in sin. The pastor advised them to put all their cares at the feet of Christ.

Paul's mother told him that she prayed that God would deliver her from a life of abuse. Eventually, she had to go into therapy to understand why she settled for a life of abuse. Paul blames his mother for her inability to save them from the abuse experienced at the hands of his father.

Central Theme

Social learning can transmit trauma to the family and community. Growing evidence shows that trauma may also be inherited epigenetically in genomic imprinting from before conception.

In other words, people can be born with trauma memories encoded in their DNA. Research evidence documents that many women exposed to domestic violence during childhood left their violent family only to enter relationships with violent partners. These women re-experience trauma and engage in a defensive reenactment of their traumatic childhood, resulting in additional trauma wounds and bruises. Intergenerational transmission (also known in the realm spirit as *generational curses*) of risks and violence occurs in families with domestic violence.

Author Commentary

Paul has experienced both betrayal and autonomy traumas. Paul has also experienced intergenerational transmission of trauma, continuing in his adult relationships the violence he survived in his childhood. Trauma has damaged Paul's sense of identity and safety.

Suggested Approach and Prayer

Paul and anyone else who has experienced a similar trauma to discover and know they can experience wholeness by embracing the following prayer declarations. When paired with the strategy to rewire your brain (chapter 11) you can begin the initial steps towards trauma wound healing, deliverance, and recovery.

- Ask to receive grace to let go of the emotional load and of trauma and take on God's easy yoke.

  His yoke is easy, and His burden is light. (Matt. 11:28–30)

- Pray that God works out forgiveness in your heart, even as He cleanses you with water and through the study of His Word.

  You are already clean because of the word I have spoken to you. (John 15:3 NIV)

- Pray to forgive the abuser even in death. Pour out all the energy that you would have used for hate, and turn direct it all in prayers to God.

> But if you do not forgive others their sins, your Father will not forgive your sins. (Matt. 6:15 NIV)

(Paul's first clinical session representing the first stage of recovery appears in chapter 9.)

Chapter 4

Trauma and Self-Worth

The devaluation may not always manifest in words, but a person's thoughts about themselves may be devaluing.

Levels of Self-Consciousness

Self-esteem is how much an individual values and sees themselves overall. Included in self-esteem is the concept of the self, which is learned. *Self-image* is how a person views themselves and the vision they have of themselves. The *ideal self* is how a person wishes they could be.[1] Research shows that what is traumatic for one person may not be the same for another, and therefore it is a person's subjective emotional experience of a traumatic event that constitutes the trauma. The higher the perception of danger as experienced by a person, the more traumatized the person will be.[2]

How a person values or devalues themselves affects how they will process a trauma experience.[3] If the person had a negative self-perception before the trauma, they may describe themselves in self-devaluing terms after experiencing a traumatic event.[4]

On a conscious level a person's self-concept contributes to one's character, feelings, motives, desires and contributes to a positive self-appraisal. Research posits that the way an individual perceives a traumatic event can either add to the disturbance or create a more developed self-appraisal system that can process and cope with extraordinary experiences.[5]

Ego States

Noted psychiatrist Eric Berne, the pioneer of the theory of transactional analysis, hypothesized that each person manifests and experiences their personality through a combination of behaviors, thoughts, and feelings using one of three "ego-states." Each ego state is a system of thinking, feeling, and behavior from which we interact with others.[6]

THE PARENT EGO STATE

The Parent ego state is one in which people's behavior is an unconscious mimicking of the actual or perceived behavior of their parents or parental figure, made up of memories formed in early childhood (from birth to the age of five) and subdivided into the Nurturing Parent and the Critical Parent.[7]

According to Dr. Eric Berne, the Nurturing Parent can be soft, loving, and permission-giving. The Critical Parent contains pre-judgments and beliefs we learned from our parents. Some of the messages held from our parents can serve us well by setting limits and boundaries, while others can be harmful.[8]

THE ADULT EGO STATE

The Adult ego State is the part of our personality that can process data accurately. It is the part that sees hears, thinks, and solves problems by utilizing information from all three ego states. A critical role of the Adult ego state is to validate data stored in the Parent ego state.[9]

THE CHILD EGO STATE

The Child ego state represents all brain recordings of internal events (feelings or emotions) similar to the ways we think and behave, linked to the external events observed during the child's first five years of life.[10]

Berne purports that the Child ego state is divided into two parts: the Free Child ego state and the Adapted, or Rebellious, Child ego state. The Child Ego state is the seat of all the feeling 'memories' we have of ourselves from childhood.

The Free Child Ego state is "spontaneous, intuitive, creative, pleasure seeker." The Adapted Child is "compliant and conforms to the wishes and demands of others, particularly parents."[11]

The Child View

According to Dr. Berne, the Child view of the world distorts the facts in a situation. A Child view prevents the Adult ego state from seeing things accurately. For example, if the child has observed or endured abuse during the first five years of life, that trauma event is lodged within the limbic system and likely to be replayed.

Parental messages viewed by the child as restricting will likely cause the child to rebel rather than comply. Parental voices are replayed and heard by the child with such statements as "You are to blame. You are bad. You are disgusting. You are no good, just like your father."

As a result of experiencing a traumatic event, victims may convey the following emotions: "I am worthless. I feel dirty and stupid. I brought this on myself. I know God is punishing me because of the lies I told my parents. I know why this happened to me; it is because I have dark skin, and I'm not as pretty as my sister."

Parental Invalidation

Parental invalidation generates helplessness and hopelessness in children. Secure adults with strong self-esteem and integrity birth secure children, emotionally unavailable parents beget anxious, avoidant children, preoccupied parents beget anxious, ambivalent children, and violence and trauma in the family will tend to create frightened, disorganized children. Parents who continuously dismiss or reject their children teach their children to disregard or distrust their emotions, relationships, and even their bodies.[12]

Childhood Trauma

Experiencing a trauma that disrupts a child's sense of safety can have a severe and long-lasting effect, including a sense of fear and helplessness which carries over into adulthood.[13]

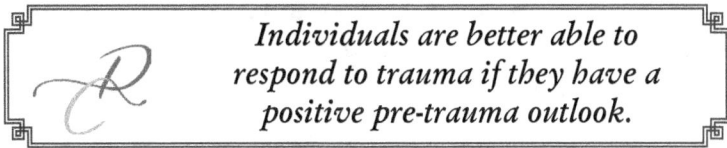

Individuals are better able to respond to trauma if they have a positive pre-trauma outlook.

Characteristics of Events That Can Lead to Trauma[14]

An event can lead to trauma if:

- It happened unexpectedly.
- You were unprepared for it.
- You felt powerless to prevent it.
- It happened repeatedly.
- Someone was intentionally cruel.
- It happened in childhood.

PRE-TRAUMA OUTLOOKS

Early-life trauma affects future self-esteem, social awareness, ability to learn, and physical health. A person who had a negative pre-trauma outlook of themselves may have their own negative core beliefs and believe, "I am not worthy of good things happening to me." After the trauma, they may strongly believe their negative view is valid.

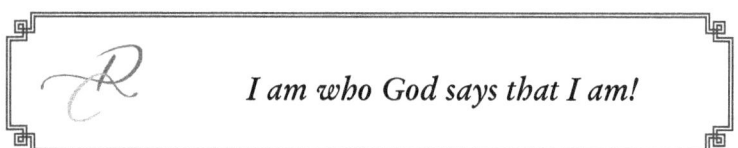

I am who God says that I am!

Different risks and protective factors, such as an individual's personality, level of resiliency, social support, and history of traumatic experiences and belief systems, can play a significant role in how the trauma is processed.[15] Individuals are better able to respond to trauma if they have a positive outlook on the world before they experience a traumatic event.[16] For example, possessing a favorable assumption about one's self, such as believing "I am who God says I am," increases one's ability to respond well to trauma.

Trauma Symptoms[17]

Emotional Reactions	Psychological Symptoms	Physical Symptoms
Shock, denial, disbelief	Confusion, difficulty concentrating	Insomnia or nightmares
Anger, irritability, mood swings	Anxiety, fear	Being easily startled
Guilt, shame, self-blame	Withdrawing from others	Racing heartbeat
Feeling sad or hopeless	Feeling disconnected or numb	Fatigue
		Difficulty concentrating
		Edginess and agitation

Chapter 5

Trauma Wounds

Early experiences involving neglect, emotional, sexual, or physical abuse, random domestic violence, and repeated abandonment create deep wounds in the soul. These wounds can be long-lasting. For instance, trauma wounds inflicted during the early developmental years can cause children to become adults who disregard or distrust their emotions and even their bodies.[1]

Injury

When we are injured, our bodies immediately go to work to heal the affected area. There are five types of open wounds to the body. Each wound is classified by its cause. Synonymous with the word *injury* are such terms as *lesion, cut, gash, laceration, tear, slash, graze, scratch, abrasion, bruise,* or *contusion*. Some trauma wounds are minor and can be treated with over-the-counter first aid. Other injuries require more than a first-aid approach to prevent infection, organ failure, and ultimately, the loss of life.

An *open wound* is created in the natural when there is an external or internal break (more substantial than a half-inch) of skin to living tissues. The skin is the first layer of protection. With this kind of wound, the bleeding does not stop by merely applying direct pressure to the wound. If the bleeding lasts longer than twenty minutes, the wound will result in severe trauma to the body.

Penetrating trauma is a type of wound that occurs when an object pierces the skin and enters a tissue of the body. The penetrating object may remain in the tissues, come back out the way it entered, or pass through the membranes and exit from another area. In *blunt or non-penetrating trauma,* there may be an impact, but the skin is not necessarily broken. In *perforating trauma*, an object enters the body and moves all the way through the skin. Perforating trauma is associated with an entrance wound and often a more massive exit wound.[2]

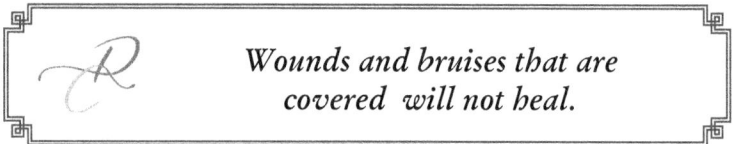

Wounds and bruises that are covered will not heal.

Just as natural wounds can differ in severity, injury to the soul resulting from an emotional trauma may also vary in severity. Taking God-inspired liberty, the medical definition of natural wounds is outlined to contextualize the mirror image of an injury to the soul based on the Trauma of Change System Model.

Abrasions and Internalized Anger

Abrasion occurs when the skin rubs or scrapes against a rough or hard exterior.[3] There's usually not much bleeding, but the wound needs to be scrubbed and cleansed to avoid infection.

Abrasions in the soul can be likened to internalized anger. Anger is a natural response to the failure of others to meet one's needs for love, praise, and acceptance. Internalized anger may be masked as repressed fear upheld by intimidating secrets, co-occurring with shame or guilt.

Figure 12

Incisions and Betrayal Trauma

An incision is a cut or a wound made by a sharp instrument or object such as a knife, shard of glass, or razor blade. Incisions bleed a lot and very quickly. A deep incision can damage tendons, ligaments, and muscles.

An incision wound in the soul is akin to *betrayal trauma*. Betrayal trauma is defined as a trauma perpetrated by someone with whom the victim is close to and reliant upon for support and survival. Betrayal trauma, particularly childhood abuse, can impair a person's self-concept, cause severe suffering, reduce daily functioning, increase risk of further victimization and perpetration of abuse, and create diverse mental health and societal problems.[4] Betrayal trauma wounds bleed into every area of self-care, in particular, establishing trust and maintaining meaningful relationships.

Lacerations and Soul Ties

A laceration is a deep cut or tearing of the skin. Accidents with knives, tools, and machinery frequently cause lacerations. The bleeding is rapid and extensive, requiring knitting of the flesh to stop the profuse bleeding.

This type of wound is akin to a soul tie with the spirit of perversion or addiction to people, things, and places. A soul tie occurs when two souls are knitted together as one flesh in the spiritual realm. Soul ties and co-dependency occur typically when ignored, shamed, or punished for expressing thoughts or feelings or for being immature, imperfect, or having needs and wants.

Puncture Wounds and Childhood Abandonment

A puncture is a small hole caused by a long, pointy object, such as a nail, needle, or ice pick. Puncture wounds may not bleed much but can be deep enough to damage internal organs.

This type of wounding is similar to childhood abandonment or neglect, which is one of the highest forms of abuse. In the United States, neglect accounts for 78 percent of all child maltreatment cases, far more than physical abuse (17 percent), sexual abuse (9 percent), and psychological abuse (8 percent) combined.

If the attachment bond was unsuccessful and traumatizing, neural dysregulation, causing an imbalance of neurological function and memories of a failed relationship, would become the basis for adult expectations of intimacy.[5]

Avulsions and Sexual Abuse

An avulsion is a partial or complete tearing away of skin and tissue. Avulsions usually occur during violent accidents, such as body-crushing accidents, explosions, and gunshots. The wound bleeds massively and rapidly.

An avulsion is likened to emotional, life-altering trauma wounds to the soul as a result of rape, incest, and sexual abuse. Such trauma tears away at the self-esteem and trust of the victimized person. If the tear in the emotional tissue remains undressed, it can last for a lifetime.

Chapter 6

Natural and Spiritual Portals

The human body is a shelter for the soul and spirit. Words spoken into the atmosphere do not just dissipate.

Words Are Matter

Every word spoken creates matter, releases energy, and travels as waves through air or empty space. Words are life. Each word represents a molecule traveling on a trajectory with increasing speed with the purpose to accomplish its aim.

Words Seek Access

God the Father created our bodies. God the Son redeemed our bodies. God the Holy Spirit dwells within our bodies. Our bodies are the very temple of the Holy Spirit of God (1 Cor. 3:16–17).

Satan battles for the soul and spirit of man and attacks the physical body with sickness, disease, and emotional bondage. The enemy desires to occupy the throne of God—your spirit, the place behind the holy of holies. Satan seeks to gain access and take up residence in our bodies. His intent, according to John 10:10, is to use that access to steal, kill, and destroy.

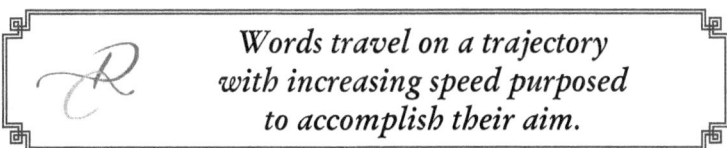

Words travel on a trajectory with increasing speed purposed to accomplish their aim.

Spiritual Portals

A spiritual portal is a doorway, gate, or entryway that allows bi-directional access from the physical world to the spirit world. Building upon quantum physics, in some sense man is a microcosm of the universe. Albert Einstein and other physicists such as Max Planck and Niels Bohr posit that we are units of matter and energy.

Satan declared in Isaiah 14:12–14 (NIV):

> "I will raise my throne above the stars of God. I will sit enthroned on the mount of the assembly, on the uttermost heights of the sacred mountain. I will ascend above the tops of the mountains. I will make myself like the Most High."

THE HUMAN BODY: AN AFFRONT TO THE ENEMY

The human body is an insult to satan on two fronts. First, mankind was made in the image and likeness of God. Secondly, the design of the body is a prototype of the Temple Mount in Jerusalem. This is the site where Jesus will return, crack the sky, and wage war in the final victory over sin and death.

TRAUMA OPENS SPIRITUAL PORTALS

Parallel portals exist both in the natural and spiritual realms. Bacteria enter our bodies through internal or external surface points that are damaged or compromised due to cuts, scrapes, or other wounds. Similarly, the enemy looks for access points to gain footholds into the soul.

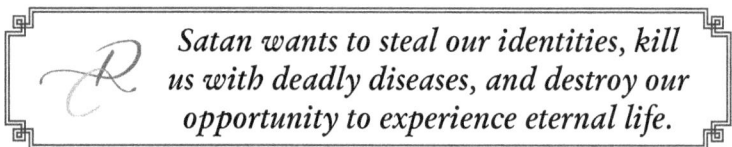

Satan wants to steal our identities, kill us with deadly diseases, and destroy our opportunity to experience eternal life.

In the spiritual or supernatural realm, a traumatic event can provide demonic spirits with legal or illegal access to one or more of the body chambers. The human body has many entry and exit portals. The ears, eyes, nose, mouth, skin, anus, urethra, cervix, sexual organs, and mammary glands are all entry and exit portals that demonic spirits can access.

Demonic spirits travel in groups. They can access one or more of the ten systems within the body. These demons, hereto referred to as *demonic squatters*, can enter the human body through open invitation or illegal entry. Upon entry, demons establish "squatter's rights" and become lodged in one or more physical organs. Once lodged in the body and spirit, demonic squatters can continue bruising, wounding, and terrorizing their host.

Parallel portals exist in the body that give entry to both the natural and the spiritual realm.

Common entry portals of trauma are:

- The use of substances
- Fornication
- Sexual abuse
- Pornography
- Trauma
- Unconfessed sins (committed by or against one's self)
- Ancient ritual practices
- Generational curses
- Adverse circumstances

The spirit of trauma provides the enemy with access to the soul. Such access affords demonic spirits a foothold and allows them to create strongholds of anger, guilt, and shame ultimately. The following is an example of how demonic squatters can gain access early through childhood trauma.

The ACE Pyramid

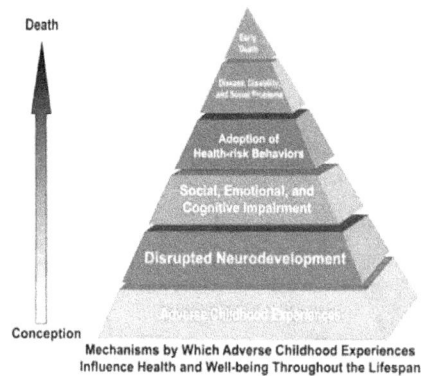

Figure 13: The CDC-Kaiser Permanente ACE Pyramid

The CDC-Kaiser Permanente Adverse Childhood Experiences (ACE) Study, conducted in the late 1990s, found an exposure that dramatically increased a person's risk of developing seven of the ten leading causes of death in the United States: severe childhood trauma. The report concluded that adverse childhood experiences in high doses could alter the structural development of neural networks and triple the exposure to chronic diseases people develop as adults. Included among chronic diseases were social and emotional problems, such as depression, becoming a perpetrator or victim of violence, and suicide.

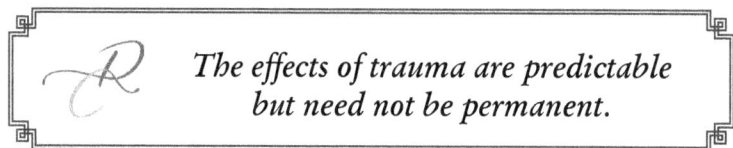

The effects of trauma are predictable but need not be permanent.

The impact of living with the threat of abuse and neglect or living with a parent who struggles with mental illness or substance abuse is associated as a dependent factor associated with high levels of adversity. These dependent factors dramatically impact health outcomes across a person's lifetime, often leading to early death.[1]

The ACE Pyramid results are predictable but not permanent. You can change the trajectory of your life. The ACE screening tool in Appendix 1 can be utilized to obtain an ACE score to determine if the enemy has accessed a portal to your soul.

Evicting Demonic Squatters

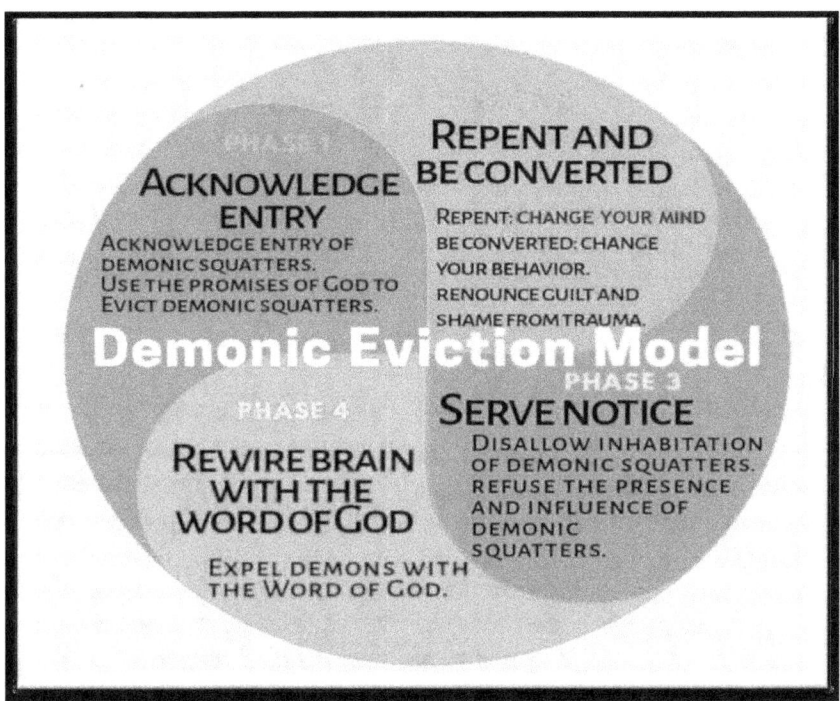

Figure 14: TOC System Model
Four Steps to Evict Demonic Squatters

STEP 1: ACKNOWLEDGE ENTRY

The first step to dislodge demonic squatters is to acknowledge their illegal or legal entry into your life. By the authority given to you as a joint heir with Jesus Christ, you can access his power and promises on earth to evict demonic squatters.

STEP 2: REPENT AND BE CONVERTED

The second step is to repent and be converted. Regardless of whether legal or illegal access was granted to demonic squatters, the next step is to repent to God. Repentance is "an inward decision or change of mind resulting in the outward action of turning from sin to God and righteousness"[2] (see Acts 20:21 KJV). Conversion is the change in thinking and behavior that follows repentance.

After you repent and are converted, you must repeatedly renounce feelings of guilt and shame related to the trauma. When repentance is linked to conversion, the spirit of trauma will leave as you resist him and join the kingdom of God.

STEP 3: SERVE NOTICE

The third step is to serve notice to the demonic squatters that you disallow their habitation in the name of Jesus and forbid any further encroachment into your life. The Holy Spirit is the discerner of truth. The brain is the central processing unit. As you refuse to tolerate the presence and influence of demonic squatters, you shall know the truth, and the truth shall set you free (John 8:32).

STEP 4: REWIRE YOUR BRAIN WITH THE WORD OF GOD

The fourth step is to rewire your brain using the Word of God. You can expel demons and rewire your brain by renewing your mind with the Word of God. Romans 12:2 explains how you can be transformed by the renewing of your mind. Satan's demons cannot share space with the Word of God in a vessel that is saved, sanctified, and submitted to Him.

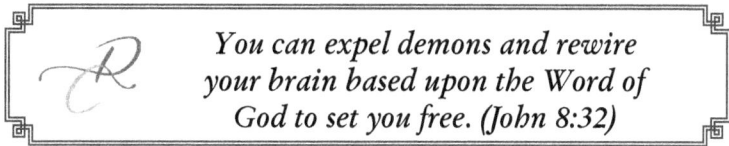

You can expel demons and rewire your brain based upon the Word of God to set you free. (John 8:32)

CHAPTER 7

Trauma Bruises: Guilt and Shame

In the natural, a bruise is an injury appearing as an area of discolored skin on the body. Bruises are caused by a blow or impact that ruptures the underlying blood vessels.[1]

In the spiritual realm, trauma leaves emotional bruises. Negative feelings of shame, fear, guilt, and blame are trauma bruises on the soul.[2] Guilt and shame are two of the most common trauma bruises. Both of these emotional wounds result from deep blows not evident to the natural eye but emotionally painful in the heart of the soul.

Examples of common negative beliefs associated with trauma include:

"I should have done something."

"I am powerless."

"I cannot protect myself."

"I am in danger."

"I am too weak."[3]

Guilt

Guilt is defined as "an unpleasant feeling with accompanying beliefs that one should have thought, felt, or acted differently."[4] Sigmund Freud said, "When we act on an idea or impulse that we later regret, we may adopt a defense mechanism of attempting to 'undo' the action to protect the ego from feelings of guilt or shame."[5] Substantial evidence suggests that intense feelings of guilt in response to an action taken or a failure to act immediately before or during a traumatic event are highly correlated with the severity of PTSD symptoms.[6] Guilt can serve as a trauma trigger, affecting a mental replay. Traumatized persons may replay events with an imagined, preferred outcome to assuage guilt.

Shame

Merriam-Webster defines *shame* as "a painful emotion caused by consciousness of guilt, shortcoming or impropriety."[7] Feelings of guilt go hand-in-hand with shame. Guilt causes a person to think, "I did something wrong"; shame causes a person to think, "I am wrong." The person begins to beat themselves up either for doing something or for not doing something. Both shame and guilt are self-conscious emotions elicited by the same kinds of adverse events.[8]

TRAUMATIC GUILT

Neuroscience research explains guilt, and shame activates similar neural circuits in the brain's reward center. Ironically, it can be appealing to heap guilt and shame on ourselves because the brain responds to these feelings with a false sense of reward.[9]

Pride, shame, and guilt all activate similar neural circuits, including the dorsomedial prefrontal cortex, amygdala, insula, and the nucleus accumbens. Pride is the most powerful of these emotions to trigger activity in these regions except the nucleus accumbens (where guilt and shame are activated in greater concentration).

FALSE RESPONSIBILITY

A victim of trauma may reach or make faulty assumptions and conclusions about the trauma. These assumptions can serve to enhance one's guilt by focusing only a positive outcome if different actions had been taken. Shame is an unpleasant feeling involving a global negative self-evaluation, taking the perspective of the others.[10]

It is common for a person experiencing a traumatic event to exacerbate feelings of shame (e.g., I should have fought back so he would have been unable to rape me).

DIFFERENCES BETWEEN GUILT AND SHAME

1. "Shame is internalized and deeply connected to our sense of who we are. . . . Guilt, on the other hand, fades with time or after corrective action is taken."

2. "Shame is based on negative assessments of a person's entire being, feeling shame can contribute to larger mental health problems."

3. "Shame does not lead to positive change" and "underlies a host of psycho-social problems: depression, substance abuse, infidelity, etc. Guilt does not."[11]

Research reveals that victims of trauma often experience a severe violation of personal boundaries which creates space for deep anger, splitting of the self, resentment, and passive-aggressive behavior.

THE REWARDS OF GUILT, SHAME, AND WORRY

It can be rewarding for one to heap guilt and shame upon themselves. In so doing, the reward center of the brain is stimulated. Ironically, worrying can help to calm the limbic system by increasing activity in the prefrontal cortex and decreasing activity in the amygdala.

Trauma Bruising of the Soul

At some point in life, we all will experience some level of wounding to the soul. We can't escape the vicissitudes of life that happen both naturally and spiritually. The spirit of trauma can infiltrate the mind with feelings of shame and guilt about one's past, and present life incapacitates the trauma victim from manifesting the glory of God wherever these feelings are found. But we can activate God's process for healing and deliverance, facilitate recovery from trauma wounds, and obtain victorious living in wholeness.

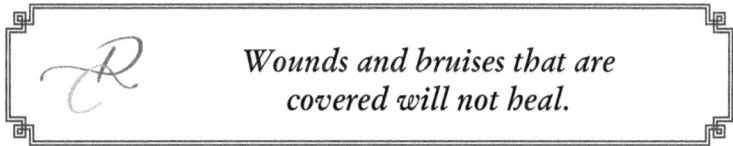

Wounds and bruises that are covered will not heal.

The following narrative of Pastor Shirley is shared to illustrate how cultivating and practicing gratitude can replace toxic feelings of guilt and shame. Pastor Shirley's narrative is an example of how the Lord is at work progressively, whether tried or challenged, amid our experiences (Heb. 6:18; Ps. 27:14).

Case #3 Trauma Narrative

Shirley is a sixty-two-year-old African American female who remembers her early childhood years as far back as the age of four. This is Shirley's account of her childhood in her own words:

What stands out for me is a memory of getting lost all of a sudden. I was separated from my mother while we were in the supermarket in Harlem, New York. When I didn't see my mother, I wandered out of the store and stood on the corner. I was scared because I didn't know where my mother was. As I stood there, a man took my hand and escorted me across the street. He asked me where I lived, and I pointed to the road across from where we were standing. This man walked me to the front of my building. I just sat on the steps of our brownstone until my mother returned.

In retrospect, I believe it was because of the Holy Spirit that the man helped me get home. When she got back to the house, my mother found me sitting on the steps. I do not know what took her so long at the store because when she got home, she had only one bag in her hand, and it was a bottle of alcohol. It was not until around age six that I realized my mother was an alcoholic.

About a year after my father died, when I was around seven, my mom remarried. Her new husband was also an alcoholic. We all moved into a two-bedroom apartment in the Bronx. I did not like my stepfather because he fondled my breasts. One time my mom had passed out next to me on my bed. My stepfather still came in and touched my breasts. He would often come into my bedroom and tickle my feet to wake me. Then he touched me in my private parts. I thought of it as a game, even though it made me uncomfortable. I was a child. Children are not sexy. I didn't understand why this was happening to me.

What stands out as a particularly horrible memory is when my stepfather tried one night to groom me for penetration. I was eight years old and frightened. He tried to force himself inside of me. He was unable to penetrate me the first time fully. At the age of thirteen, I finally told my mom. Her response was, "You must have liked it." I don't know if it was the alcohol talking, but I couldn't believe my mother said those words to me.

I went into a tailspin of confusion. It lasted many years of my life and resulted in years of abusive relationships. I accepted Christ as my Lord and Savior when I was seventeen years old at a local church. During an evening service, I just threw my burdens and pain at the altar. I needed so much deliverance. I was a perpetual backslider for many years. I thank God for His grace and mercy that rescued me. Knowing how much God had done for me helped set me on a committed path toward healing.

One night I had a dream that my stepfather was going to hell. I was not happy that he was going to hell, but I was still emotionally numb. I began to study the Scriptures more and regularly attend church in an attempt to ask God to forgive me for hating the ones who had hurt me. I knew I would have to confront the trauma of abuse and the pain both of my parents inflicted.

Twenty years ago, when I was around forty-two years old, my stepfather became sick. I went to visit him and my mother in the apartment where years of abuse occurred. I hated going there because of the memories. At that point in my adult journey, I was saved but still not entirely delivered. During my visit with my stepfather, I asked if I could pray for him. He said yes. I told him about the thief on the cross and the mercy of God toward him. After I prayed for him, I felt as if hot oil was being poured over me from the top of my head and dripping down all over me.

After that experience, I wept for several days. I asked the Lord what had happened. He said it was a touch of His compassion. The oil of the altar, the place of sacrifice, soothed my broken life. I left the hatred behind me. Now my heart is where the love of God dwells.

A few months later my stepfather was in the hospital hooked to a ventilator. During all this time, the Lord was dealing with me and all of my secret sins and hidden issues. I went to see him, and the devil reminded me of the trauma. Even as I proceeded to minister to my stepfather, I could visualize his hand touching me. The sexual sensation in my private part and the smell of alcohol on his breath all came back to me. In the hospital room with my stepfather, I pressed forward. Feeling the strength of the Holy Spirit, I took him by the hand saying, "I forgive you for all of the horrible things you did to me. I am saved now, and the Word of God says that for me to be forgiven I also have to forgive."

I spoke to him about repentance and led him into a prayer for salvation. As I continued to pray, he faded in and out of consciousness. I recited the sinner's prayer and said, "If you agreed with what I just prayed, just squeeze my hand." He squeezed my hand, and the next day he died.

For many years after his death, I dealt with feelings of shame and guilt. A part of me thought the abuse was my fault. However, through the love of God that surpasses our understanding, I have victory over it. The Lord has entirely saved and sanctified me, and I have accepted the call to pastoral ministry. It is so amazing how God will give you beauty for ashes. I am so amazed at how God chooses to heal. To God be the glory!

Central Theme

The central theme of chapter 7 is how feelings of guilt go hand-in-hand with shame. Both emotions activate identical neural circuits in the brain's reward center. We respond to these feelings with a false sense of reward.

The pastor in this narrative experienced the first phase in the cycle of change towards trauma healing, deliverance, and recovery by acknowledging the trauma and fear. The reader can draw hope from Shirley's experience that healing from the wounds of trauma is possible. When paired with the strategy to rewire your brain (chapter 10), you can begin the initial steps towards trauma wound healing and deliverance and promote recovery. Gratitude unshackles us from toxic emotions and has a lasting effect on the brain.

Prayer Focus:

Shirley and anyone else who has experienced similar traumas can practice gratitude to replace feelings of guilt and shame. Embracing the following prayer declarations will set your mind to identify the positive things in yourself and your life. Repeat the following prayer declarations aloud. Add your own declarations of appreciation and repeat them daily.

- Lord, I thank you that you saved me and helped me to understand the power of love and forgiveness.
- Thank you for the opportunity to share my testimony with others.
- I am grateful for surviving that which was designed to kill me.
- Thank you for renewing my mind daily.

Chapter 8

Deliverance, Healing, and Recovery

Often behind a stronghold there is a framework of trauma. Strongholds are the ways demonic squatters use to manifest as a mindset contrary to the Word of God or sickness or disease in any part of the eleven systems in the body.

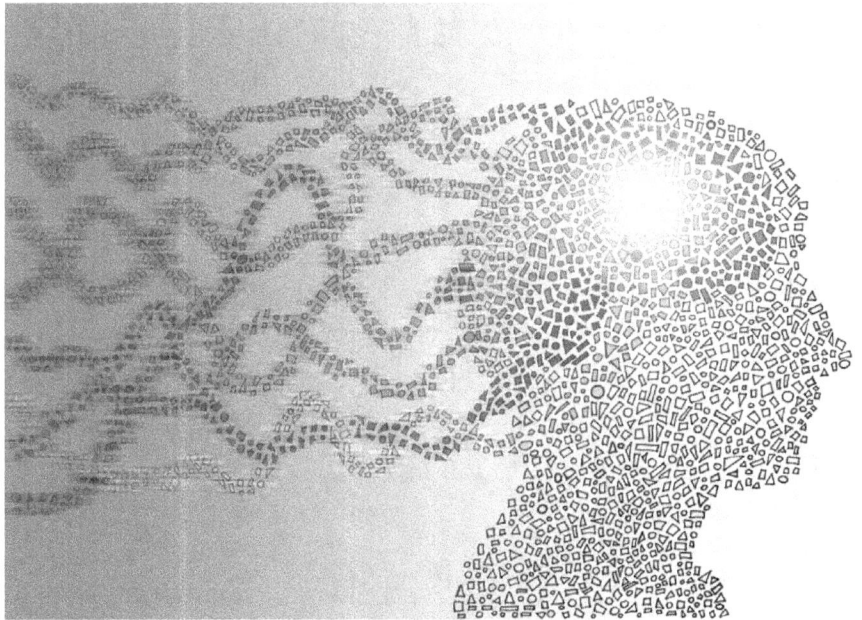

Figure 14

Salvation

Is Required for Deliverance

The escape from demonic influences in this world system can only be obtained through salvation. According to God's written Word, salvation is the ransom which was paid for by Jesus Christ and occurs when one is saved by the grace of God. One must believe that Jesus healed the brokenhearted, delivered the captives from bondage and fear, recovered sight to the blind, and set at liberty them that are bruised.

All aspects of deliverance and salvation are available only through the person and work of Jesus Christ, who was Himself delivered up for us (Rom. 4:25) so that we would be delivered from eternal punishment for sin.[153]

Is an Exchange of Traumas

Salvation is an exchange of your trauma for God's healing, deliverance, and freedom. Jesus experienced every possible trauma on earth. He experienced betrayal (1 Cor. 11:23), felt shame (Heb. 12:2), and physical and emotional abuse (John 19:1–4). Jesus endured all of this and carried our griefs and sorrows (Isa. 53:4) once and for all at the cross.

Is Available Now

We are born in sin. Salvation is the first step toward deliverance. The traumatic events sent by satan were attempts to separate you from God, weaken your body, damage relationships, disrupt healthy thought patterns, and drive you into despair. Perhaps you have been under the effects of trauma until now.

Healing is immediately available to you if you embrace it. You've already made the decision to choose to heal by reading this book. You don't have to suffer from traumatic memories and strongholds. The penalty of sin has already been paid by Jesus.

You need not be in a church or religious setting to receive salvation. Let's take the next step of salvation together. Salvation is as easy as A, B, C:

A: Accept Jesus Christ as Lord and Savior.

B: Believe in your heart that God raised Jesus from the dead.

C: Confess with your mouth that you are a sinner and you shall be saved.

God's plan for our salvation has three parts, in this order: *justification, sanctification, and glorification*. One must believe that Jesus became the propitiation for mankind and deliver us from the penalty of sin and death. Justification is God's unconditional love for us through Jesus Christ's death on the cross.

Sanctification is the reciprocation of our love toward Jesus. Glorification is the ultimate reward we'll receive when Jesus returns.

> That if thou shalt confess with thy mouth the Lord Jesus, and shalt believe in thine heart that God hath raised him from the dead, thou shalt be saved. For with the heart man believeth unto righteousness, and with the mouth confession is made unto salvation. (Rom. 10:9–10)

Confess: Jesus, I believe You died on the cross for my sins. I confess You as my Lord and Savior. Forgive me of my sins. I forgive and release all who have sinned against me. I receive salvation. Strengthen me to walk through each stage of healing, deliverance, and recovery from trauma. In the name of Jesus. Amen.

Deliverance

In the Word of God

The word *deliverance* occurs in the Old Testament 149 times in 25 books. In the New Testament, the word *deliverance* occurs 32 times in 13 books. The thrust of Christ's ministry about man's deliverance is mentioned twice in the Bible.

Old Testament:

> The Spirit of the Lord God is upon me; because the Lord hath anointed me to preach good tidings unto the meek; he hath sent me to bind up the brokenhearted, to proclaim liberty to the captives, and the opening of the prison to them that are bound. (Isaiah 61:1)

New Testament: The first mention is in the Gospel of Luke:

> The Spirit of the Lord is upon me, because he hath anointed me to preach the gospel to the poor; he hath sent me to heal the brokenhearted, to preach deliverance to the captives, and recovering of sight to the blind, to set at liberty them that are bruised. (Luke 4:18)

The second time *deliverance* is found in the New Testament is in the book of Hebrews:

> Women received back their dead, raised to life again. There were others who were tortured, refusing to be released so that they might gain an even better resurrection. (Heb. 11:35 NIV)

Is God's Rescue

Within a biblical context, *deliverance* refers to the acts of God whereby he rescues his people from their enemies (1 Sam. 17:37; 2 Kings 20:6) ("snatch away") and from the hand of the wicked (Psalm 7:2; 17:13; 18:16– 19; 59:2; 69:14; 71:4) ("make an escape," "to cause to escape," to "draw out," and "to save").[1]

From Strongholds

One aspect of deliverance deals with demonically caused psychological and physical conditions. The demonic strongholds created by psychological and physical diseases must be dismantled through the spiritual process of deliverance.

An example of a psychological stronghold can be viewed through the maladaptive behavior of prostitution. Sixty-six percent of prostitutes were abused by their father or father figures.[2] Prostitution is manifested in the kingdom of darkness through activities of the four angels of prostitution, (succubi, demonic entities inciting sexual gnosis)[3] who gain access to the soul often through the spirit of trauma.

This behavior counters the truth of God's Word found in Romans 12:1:

> I beseech you, therefore, brethren, by the mercies of God,
> that ye present your bodies a living sacrifice, holy, acceptable
> unto God, which is your reasonable service.

The escape from demonic occupation and influences in this world system can only be obtained through salvation made available through Jesus Christ.

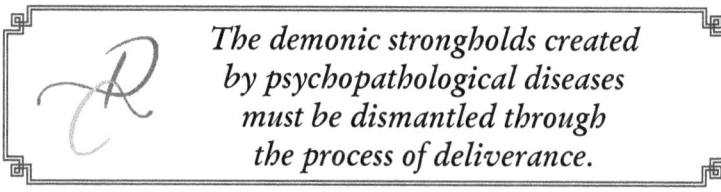

The demonic strongholds created by psychopathological diseases must be dismantled through the process of deliverance.

TEMPORAL DELIVERANCE VERSUS SPIRITUAL DELIVERANCE

God's removal of those who are in the midst of trouble or danger deals mainly with liberation or temporal deliverance from demonically caused mental and physical conditions.[4]

As previously stated, God does rescue His people from their enemies and from the hand of the wicked. The descriptions of temporal deliverance in the Old Testament serve as symbolic representations of the *spiritual deliverance* from sin. Deliverance from sin (as described in the New Testament) is only available through Christ and granted to those who accept by faith God's conditions of repentance and faith in Jesus Christ.

Jesus offers spiritual deliverance from "mankind's greatest peril—sin, evil, death, and judgment." Believers are delivered once for all time according to the word of God, from eternal punishment, by God's power, from this present evil age (Gal. 1:4) and from the power of satan's reign (Col. 1:13).[5]

HEALING AND DELIVERANCE

Deliverance and healing is a restorative process involving the regaining of possession or control of something stolen to a former and better state of wholeness. Healing from the emotional wounds of trauma is akin to *temporal* deliverance. The Lord delivers the believer from the trials of this life.

He uses trials to mature us in the faith, (seemingly no matter how many trips are made to the altar). "For our present troubles are small and won't last very long. Yet they produce for us a glory that vastly outweighs them and will last forever!" (2 Cor. 4:17 NLT). God makes the way of escape in His perfect will and timing, after patience has had its perfect work (James 1:2–4, 12).

DELIVERANCE BEGINS IN THE MIND

The method of temporal deliverance begins in the mind and is concretized through the words we release out of the mouth gate with speech.

The brain takes the shape the mind rests upon. Our brains are plastic (we can direct it, and it can grow in that direction); we rewire it to look for rewards and not be threatened. Deliverance is enforced with the words spoken and released out of your mouth in alignment with the Word of God. God is complemented when we behave and speak like Him.

The process of deliverance often consists of three main parts: (1) tearing down strongholds, (2) removing legal rights with the Word of God, and (3) casting out the remaining demons.[6]

Higher Ground

Mankind is a speaking spirit. Words matters, for they create life and death (Prov. 18:21). Speech is the conduit of thought. The higher order of speech, the greater the outcome. Man's speech is the first line of defense toward the process of deliverance.

Victory is attainable when one decrees life-sustaining words in alignment with the Word of God. If you change how you think based on the Word of God, you will change how you speak and feel. Your mind and your faith will respond to anything you say.

Deliverance Is Commissioned

In the New Testament Gospels, "Jesus never commissioned anyone to preach the Gospel without also commanding them to minister healing and deliverance."[7] He told them "As you go to heal the sick, cast out demons." (Matthew 10:1, 7–8). The key action verb is that as you go to heal the sick, "cast out demons." Deliverance must occur first, and healing will become a follower. Satan's demons cannot share space with the Spirit of God in a vessel that is saved, sanctified, and submitted to Him. *Sanctified* and *submitted* are the operative words.

The Trauma of Change System Model

The spirit of trauma affects the circuitry of the brain, leaving victims of trauma disabled with terrorizing memories. The good news is that, according to research, a person can rewire the brain and rebuild areas affected by trauma. The Trauma of Change System Model (TOC), conceptualized by the author under the leading of the Holy Spirit, is introduced in this segment of the book to inform the reader how one can repair brain function and achieve higher order brain activity after a traumatic assault.

Wire What You Desire

The Trauma of Change System Model integrates the best of neuroscience, psychology, physiology, and biblio-neurotechnology, to activate core spiritual states of healing, deliverance, and recovery. The strategies described in the TOC system can assist victims of trauma to improve higher-order brain activity and leverage evidence-based neuroscience strategies to rewire the brain. The Word of God lets us know that we can retrain our mind and be transformed through the renewing of the mind. This systematic approach described in the model has a dual objective: (1) to activate deliverance from the spirit of trauma; and (2) to catapult healing and facilitate the recovery process.

Four Phases of Deliverance Process

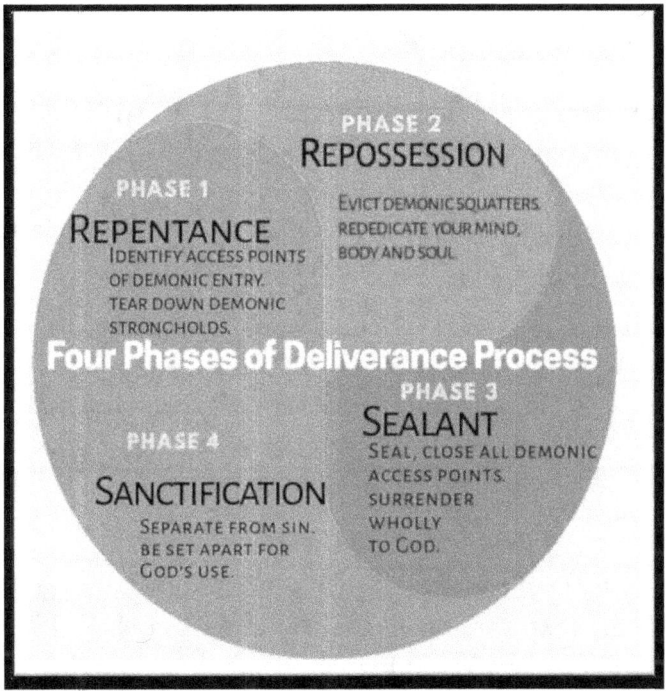

Figure 15: Trauma of Change System Model Four Phases of Deliverance Process

TOC Repentance: Phase 1 of Deliverance

The first phase of deliverance processing is the forward step involving repentance. Identify the access point which allowed legal or illegal access through a portal to the temple. Repent from sins of omission and of commission.

Repentance is an inward decision (by believers) or a change of mind resulting in the outward action of "turning from sin to God and righteousness" (Act 21:20). Repentance means to shift from the wrong way to the right direction. You leave the kingdom of satan and join the kingdom of God.[8] Repentance leads to conversion, which is demonstrated by changed behaviors and practices. Repentance and conversion are followed by the tearing down of strongholds (deceptive thought patterns and behaviors). After you have repented and been converted, renounce the spirit of trauma.

TOC: Repossession Phase 2 of Deliverance

The second phase of deliverance processing involves evicting demonic squatters from your earthly temple to be set free from the spirit of trauma. You must decide to see yourself free and confess the truth of the Word that you already have eternal victory over satan and demonic spirits through Jesus Christ.

Use the authority given to believers as joint heirs with Jesus Christ to access His power and promises (which is available) to evict demonic squatters. During this deliverance phase, notification is given in the name of Jesus to the demonic squatters that you disallow their habitation and forbid any further encroachment into your life.

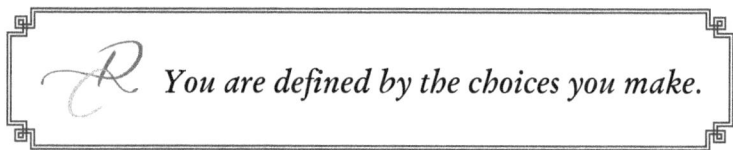

You are defined by the choices you make.

TOC: Sealant Phase 3 of Deliverance

The third phase of deliverance processing involves locating and shutting portals or doors that were opened. These doors may have been opened generationally or in present time.

Regardless of the origin of the point of entry, these open doors allow demonic squatters legal or illegal access to your body temple. Shut all open portal doors in fervent warfare prayer.

Unless you close those doors, the devil has a legal right to steal, kill, and destroy you. If you fail to close these doors, the devil has a constitutional right to operate in your life. Satan will exert this right and continue to steal, kill, and destroy any blessing that is in your life. Seal the entrance portal permanently by rededicating your life to God as one of holiness. (Appendix 3 contains daily warfare declaration prayers to rehearse and speak aloud.)

TOC: SANCTIFICATION PHASE 4 OF DELIVERANCE

The fourth phase of deliverance processing involves sanctification. Sanctification is separation from the seduction of sin involving the restoration or salvation of the soul.

Sanctify yourselves, therefore, and be ye holy: for I am the Lord your God. And ye shall keep my statutes, and do them: I am the Lord which sanctify you. (Leviticus 20:7–8)

MAKE A DECISION

What you will not confront and decide to speak to will continually confront you. Brain science reveals when you make a decision, your brain feels it has control.

Making a "decision" includes *identifying and choosing alternatives*, *creating intentions*, and *setting goals*. All three parts of decision making are part of the same neural circuitry and engage the prefrontal cortex, positively by reducing worry and anxiety.[9]

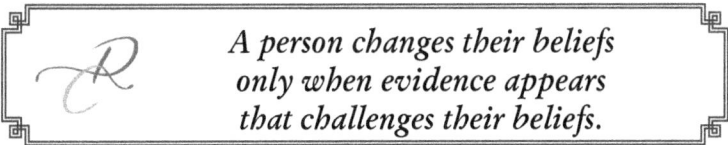

A person changes their beliefs only when evidence appears that challenges their beliefs.

YOU MUST ACKNOWLEDGE THE PROBLEM

I help clients in my practice to increase their level of self-awareness by supporting the perspective that each person influences what they choose to believe and how they want to show up in life each day. As a clinician, I operate from the premise that *I do not have to believe what a client believes about a thing, but I do have to believe they believe it.*

When a person experiences trauma, their assumptions may be shattered. This leads to confusion and distress as the person struggles to make sense of what has happened. It is not uncommon for a person to alter their belief with a new, disabling one to rationalize a traumatic event. As the new, contrary belief strengthens, dysfunctional beliefs begin to trump existing positive beliefs.

Dysfunctional beliefs about the trauma event and the person's ability to thwart the experience are imprinted by satan and upheld as a truth. People do not change their beliefs because someone else thinks they should. A person changes their thinking about a thing when new evidence appears that contradicts and challenges their own beliefs. Unresolved traumas intertwined with dysfunctional beliefs can hinder the healing and recovery process, resulting in psychopathology.

Chapter 9

Healing Trauma Wounds and Bruises

Mankind was made in the image and likeness of God.

THE IMAGE OF GOD

On the last day of creation, "God said, 'Let us make man in our image, after our likeness. And let them have dominion over the fish of the sea and over the birds of the heavens and over the livestock and over all the earth and over every creeping thing that creeps on the earth'" (Gen. 1:26 ESV). Being made in the "image" of God means we were made to resemble God, for "God is a Spirit" (John 4:24) and man is a "speaking spirit" based on some translations of the phrase "living soul" in Genesis 2:7.

HEALING ENERGY

The body is an energy system. At the cellular level, the system is self-directed and thought-affected. Energy usage works alike a sinkhole: energy goes where it is needed in the body.[1] The mind replays past events and announces events of your future by combining the past, present, and future perspectives to balance life.[2] These experiences are etched as data processed and stored within the computer chip.

PHASES OF PHYSIOLOGIC WOUND HEALING

The healing that occurs through natural body processes is God in action. In the natural realm, wound healing is the physiologic restoration of structure and function of injured or diseased tissues. The healing processes include blood clotting, tissue mending, scarring, and bone healing. Wound healing is a complex process of biochemical reactions and cellular events in which the skin, and the tissues under it, repairs tissue after injury.[3]

Motivational Forces

The immune cells are the chief orchestrators of healing.[4] Extrinsic motivation arises from outside of the individual. Intrinsic motivation stems from within because it is naturally satisfying to you. It is critical to remember that physical wound healing is not linear, and often, emotional trauma wound healing can progress both forward and back through the phases depending upon intrinsic and extrinsic motivational forces.[5]

The man at the pool of Bethesda vacillated between intrinsic and extrinsic motivation. His presence at the pool (a place where healing takes place) indicates that he had a desire for healing, yet the response given to Jesus did not reflect the man as having intrinsic motivation.

Extrinsic forces are at play when we are motivated to perform a behavior or engage in an activity to earn a reward or avoid punishment. Intrinsic motivation involves participating in action because it is personally rewarding, essentially, acting for its own sake rather than the desire for some external reward.

The Decision Is Yours

Life is a journey, and each day you can decide how you want to show up and make history. Healing can include relief from spiritual, physical, emotional, mental, and demonic oppression. You can decide whether you want to live as a victim or a victorious warrior on the battlefield for the Lord.

The Four Phases of Physical Wound Healing

When a person experiences physical trauma, the skin, which is the largest organ in your body, begins four phases of wound healing: homeostasis, inflammation, proliferation, and remodeling.

1. **Homeostasis Phase** is the first phase of wound healing.[6] Platelets–blood cells that are critical in forming clots–aggregate at the damaged site and initiate clot formation to prevent blood loss and create a temporary covering that protects the external environment.

2. **Inflammatory Phase** is the second phase and the body's natural response to injury.[7] While the platelets aggregate together, they also secrete factors that recruit other immune cells. These factors initiate the inflammatory phase.

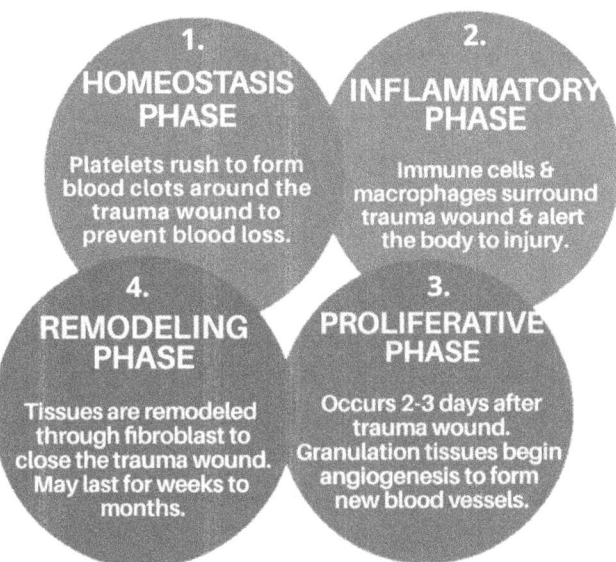

Figure 16

After initial wounding, the blood vessels in the wound bed contract and a clot is formed. The redness and swelling which appears during the inflammation stage occur as a result of the dilation of local blood vessels, which allow immune cells to enter the damaged site. Inflammation is your body's way of alerting you of an injury.

The next wave of immune cells to arrive at the scene includes monocytes and can be mobilized in response to injury or infection. Once in the wound, these cells can differentiate into cells called macrophages, the immune system's "construction workers." These macrophages use their "eating" capacity to clear the damaged site of debris and remove foreign material and bacteria from the wound. This lays the foundations for tissue repair and coordinates the wound healing response.

3. **Proliferative phase** is the third phase of wound healing.[8] It occurs between two to three days after the wound occurs. This phase resolves the inflammatory phase, and the period where the wound contracts as new tissues are rebuilt. When inflammation occurs, the body releases several kinds of cells, including those that are responsible for migration and proliferation.

During proliferation, the wound is "rebuilt" with new granulation tissue, which is comprised of collagen and extracellular matrix and into which a new network of blood vessels develops, a process known as angiogenesis, which involves the formation of new blood vessels.

Once the bleeding is under control, the body then begins the process of rebuilding tissue. Restoration of tissue continuity occurs initially without granulation accomplished by wound closure filling with granulation tissue.

4. **Remodeling phase** is the final phase which occurs once the wound has closed. It involves "tissue remodeling, which can persist for weeks to months. The extracellular matrix hastily laid down by fibroblasts in the proliferative phase is not meant to be permanent. Its production, and the swift wound-closure that accompanied it, are simply stopgap measures to prevent blood loss and infection."[9] Although the wound is closed at this point, the tissue is not entirely back to normal.

The temporary closure or scab that forms on the surfaces of the wound during the proliferative phase is not meant to be permanent.

Granulation tissue typically grows from the base of a wound and can fill wounds of almost any size. Its production and the swift wound-closure that accompanied it are merely stopgap measures to prevent blood loss and infection. Cellular activity reduces and the number of blood vessels in the wounded area regress and decrease.

Healing Disease and Recovering from Illness

Medical research reveals that one heals from disease and one recovers from an illness.[10] The disease can be mental, spiritual, or physical. As in the natural realm of healing, there are mirror components to the process of deliverance, healing, and recovery. The healing process is viewed as restoring balance—balance within the individual's total well-being.

Healing Toward Wholeness

Healing is the body's natural process of repairing damage caused by physical or psychological trauma and the method of combating the disease.[11] Healing involves movement toward an experience of integrity and wholeness in response to an injury or illness. It literally meaning to make whole, the restoration of health to an unbalanced, diseased, or damaged organism.[12]

HIGHER-LEVEL HEALING

In the realm of the Spirit, healing can manifest when you superimpose the Word of God over disabling patterns of "low level" negative thoughts, neutralizing their frequency to achieve a higher level of thinking.

DECIDE TO BE HEALED

Life is a journey, and each day you can decide how you want to show up and make history. Healing in the realm of the Spirit is a choice that involves a shift in the energy or faith based on the Word of God generated by conscious and unconscious processes. The very act of thinking is neuro-technology. To know, decide, and understand are cognitive functions that involve the prefrontal lobe of the brain, modulation of neurons, and sensory information input. The frontal lobes of our brain work in tandem with the limbic system to influence our experience and the response to the experience.

Decreasing the Impact of Trauma

Research has demonstrated that individuals who detail their past traumatic experiences decrease their autonomic reactivity and subjective experience of distress, stimulate productive behavioral change, enhance their immune function, and improve their physical health over time.[13]

Writing about trauma can decrease automatic triggers, responses, and negative feelings. Suppression of emotional thought decreases immune functioning. Keeping significant traumatic experiences private or hidden is associated with increased rates of disease, rumination, and subjective distress.[14]

In psychiatry and psychology, healing is the process by which neuroses and psychoses are resolved to the degree that the client can lead a healthy or fulfilling existence without being overwhelmed by psycho-pathological phenomena.[15] In other words, healing from the spirit of trauma allows one to function beyond the impact of traumatic experiences.

BACKGROUND PROGRAMS

To heal psychological and emotional trauma, you must figure out what programs are still running in the background of your mind and reduce the impact of adverse memories.

Thoughts running in the background are often "on replay" and generally reflect those things we are trying to make sense of in the trauma experience. You can't make sense out of a senseless act; you will have to shut down the replay. Every time we recall an added feature not initially associated with the memory, it now becomes part of the scenario.[16]

Narrative Memory

Trauma healing and treatment involves processing trauma-related memories. Research suggests controlling the condition under which traumatic memories are recalled, using the technique referred to as *narrative memory*, can change their content.[17] Using a narrative memory technique, you can rewrite the trauma experience and visualize the outcome that yields a more favorable outcome.[18] Visualization of what you want to see and remember is critical, and the process primes the brain. You can actually use visualization to create the emotion you want to experience. The stronger the emotion, the stronger the mental map.

Writing to Rewrite

Writing is a psycho-muscular activity that involves a collection of cells in the base of your brain known as the reticular activating system (RAS). The RAS is the filter for all of the information your brain needs to process, and it gives more attention to what you are currently focusing on.[19] The word of God provides the first step on how to remove and replace the memory of the trauma. Write the vision that you want to see and make it plan.

> Brethren, I count not myself to have apprehended: but this one thing I do, forgetting those things which are behind, and reaching forth unto those things which are before, I press toward the mark for the prize of the high calling of God in Christ Jesus. (Philippians 3:13–14)

The Trauma of Change System Model – Wound Triage Treatment

The Trauma of Change System Model can be retrofitted to the first phase of treatment for a physical wound. Treatment precedes healing within the supernatural and natural realms.

The initial triage of a wound is followed by treatment which also may include intense surgery and aftercare. If an object is deeply embedded in the skin or muscle, removing a sharp instrument from the skin or muscle may cause additional damage.

Likewise, mental attempts made to disassociate from the memory of a trauma experience will manifest in behavioral forms and create new destructive mental maps.

Some wounds in the natural are minor and therefore can respond to minimal treatment with an over-the-counter, first-aid approach. Emotional trauma wounds require more than a first-aid approach to forestall demonic encroachment and dismantle the foul ground. When you possess an unshakable mentality and prevailing belief that you are no longer a victim but victorious through Jesus Christ, you can safely transition into the first phase of trauma healing stage processing.

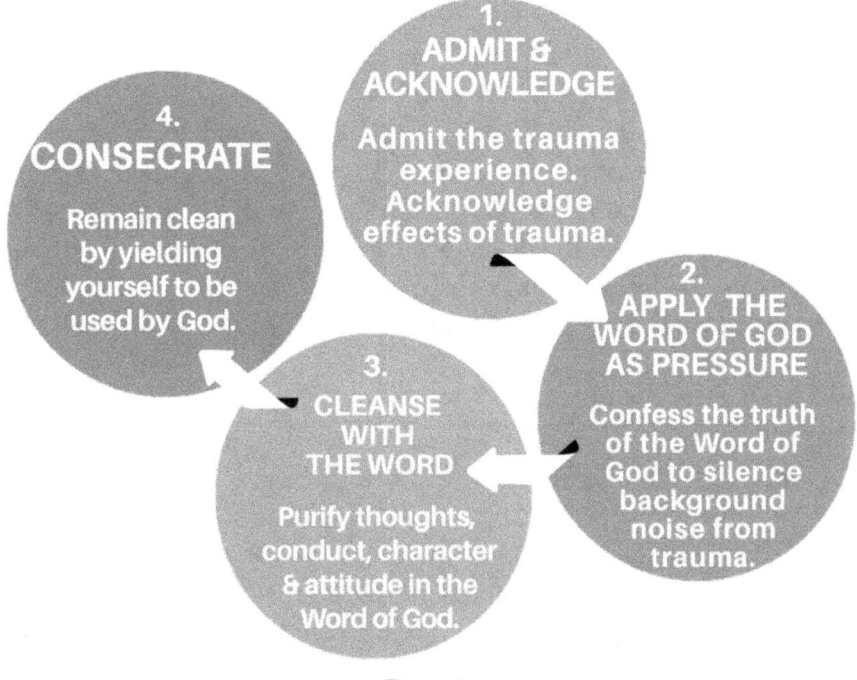

Figure 17

STEP 1: ADMIT AND ACKNOWLEDGE THE TRAUMA WOUND

The first step is to admit that the trauma experience happened and still affects you. "If we confess our sins, He is faithful and just to forgive us our sins, and to cleanse us from all unrighteousness" (1 John 1:9).

The process of deliverance, healing, and recovery will not happen overnight. However, by making a conscious decision to superimpose a positive thought over the negative one, it will provide a locus of control, creating a new mental map to the extent to which individuals believe they can control events affecting them. The individual will have to take control over that which is trying to control them.

Step 2: Apply the Word to the Trauma Wound

The second step is to apply the Word of God to the trauma wound. Applying firm, direct pressure and elevating the wound controls bleeding and swelling. You would continue to use force with sterile gauze or a clean cloth until the bleeding stops. Hebrews 10:23 (NLT) says to "hold tightly without wavering to the hope we affirm, for God can be trusted to keep his promise." Holding tightly to the promises of God for total healing can drown out the background noise struggling to be in the first-place position.

Step 3: Cleanse the Wound with the Word

The third step is to clean and protect the wound by washing and disinfecting it with water to remove all dirt and debris. Water is a universal solvent and is symbolic of the Holy Spirit. In Ephesians 5:26, the apostle Paul tells us that we are cleansed "with the washing of water by the word." When we study the Word and declare the Word, it will purify our thoughts, conduct, character, and attitude.

Step 4: Consecrate

The fourth step is to wrap the wound to keep it from exposure to germs. Leviticus 20:7 says, "Sanctify yourselves therefore, and be ye holy: for I am the Lord your God." You will need to keep the wound clean and dry by consecrating yourself to the Lord. You can do this by simply saying, "Lord Jesus, I am for you. I'm no longer for myself, the world, or anything else. I am for your use and your satisfaction."

The Trauma of Change System Model posits that words in opposition to the Word of God can manifest in destructive thoughts, beliefs, values, and principles. Words spoken in opposition to the truth of God's Word will forestall the stage processing phase of healing and deliverance. Your cells respond to everything you say or think.

Recovery and salvation is a restorative process of regaining possession or control of something stolen or lost, thus allowing us to return to a former and better state of wholeness. The Word of God and His promises found in Scripture are constructive, growth-oriented, and fueling. The Word of God builds new thoughts, habits, and mental maps, releases endorphins, and facilitates healing.

When you follow the four steps outlined to treat and clean the wound, you will be positioned to activate one or more components in the multi-stage processing phase of **The Trauma of Change System Model**.

Paul's Session Notes

The first step towards a process of recovery is to acknowledge the issue and face it. The following session notes demonstrate Paul's first step to confronting a traumatic memory of witnessing intimate partner violence and experiencing childhood sexual abuse and abandonment.

On a Monday morning in the fall of 2015, Paul arrived at the Rapid Recovery Center Clinic with his girlfriend, Diane, and approached the reception counter for a 3:00 p.m. appointment. He asked to see Dr. Charles, and the receptionist presented him with a clipboard of intake information for him to complete. She asked him to complete all the attached forms, and Paul replied by saying, "All of these damn forms?" The receptionist responded, "Yes, all of them. It's a HIPAA requirement. Make sure you sign the front and the back of each form, please."

Paul murmured and cursed under his breath as he completed the forms in the waiting room with Diane. He returned the clipboard and slammed it on the counter. The receptionist acknowledged him and told him that the doctor would be with him in a moment.

As Diane waited in the reception area, Paul came into my office. The following is an account of our exchange.

Dr. Charles: Hello, Paul, what brings you in today?

Paul: My mother suggested that I see you because you were helpful to her.

Dr. Charles: Tell me more.

Paul: More about what?

Dr. Charles: Why your mother suggested that you come to the Center for Rapid Recovery.

Paul: She thinks I need help like she did when my father used to beat her. That is why she came to see you. Don't you remember?

Dr. Charles: I don't know your mother, and even if I did, I couldn't talk to you about her without authorization.

Paul murmured something unintelligible under his breath.

Dr. Charles: We don't have to talk about your mother. Let's talk about what you remember about your mother's abuse.

Paul: You should know. She came here for treatment. Read her records.

Dr. Charles: Once again, Paul, I can't confirm or deny whether or not your mother received treatment. Didn't you mention that you were referred to the center by your mother?

Paul: Yeah.

Dr. Charles: How old were you when your mother was allegedly abused by your father?

Paul: Allegedly abused? Are you f-N crazy? He came home drunk and beat her—every day—and his d--- son raped me. I begged her to leave, but she wouldn't.

Dr. Charles: I can see the memory of the encounter between your mother and father stirs up intense emotions for you.

Paul: Damn right, lady.

Dr. Charles: How old were you when you witnessed the abuse?

Paul: Oh, now you can see this as abuse, like I was lying.

Dr. Charles: No, Paul, I can see by your response that it was a real experience for you. I just want to be cautious of violating any HIPAA laws.

Paul: F--- the law. I wouldn't be sitting here if it wasn't for my mother putting up with the abuse from my father. Now I'm acting just like his a--.

Dr. Charles: Tell me more, Paul.

Paul: I'm tired. Why don't you just look at her chart and read all about it?

Dr. Charles: How would you feel if I asked your mother to come in and meet with us for your next visit?

Paul: Who said that I was coming back?

Dr. Charles: Would you like to find out why you are acting like your father, as you mentioned?

Paul: I don't want to be like him. I hate him, and I hate her for allowing him to make me like this.

Dr. Charles: Let's meet with your mother, and maybe she can shed some light on why she allowed it. What's your thought about that?

Paul: Yeah, I want to know.

Dr. Charles: Great! I just have a few more questions before you go.

Paul: (In an angry tone) What else do you want to know?

Dr. Charles: Do you use drugs or drink alcohol?

Paul: Yeah, I drink sometimes.

Dr. Charles: Have you ever had thoughts of committing suicide or killing someone?

Paul: Yes.

Dr. Charles: Tell me more about your thoughts of committing suicide or killing someone?

Paul: It was just a thought, and I wouldn't do it, and that's it! Everyone thinks about ending it at some point. It doesn't mean I would do it.

Dr. Charles: Yes, that may be true, but there is a difference in a thought process and planning. My question relates to whether you ever had a plan and method of killing yourself or someone else.

Paul: Listen, lady, I told you. I wouldn't kill myself or anyone else. If I did want to kill someone, it would be my father and his abusive son, John. My father is dead, and John is in prison getting what is due to him for sexually abusing me. I'm out of here.

Dr. Charles: I would like to talk to you more about how you resolved some of those thoughts.

Paul: I am through talking to you.

Dr. Charles: OK, let's plan on getting your mother in here to shed some light on why she allowed your father to be abusive. When do you want to come back with your mother?

Paul: Next Monday at 3:00 p.m.

Dr. Charles: I look forward to continuing our conversation, Paul. Please feel free to contact me in between sessions if something comes up. Do you have my number? Goodbye.

Paul: I won't be calling before next Monday. Goodbye.

Note: To heal from psychological and emotional trauma, you must face and resolve the unbearable feelings and memories you've long avoided. Trauma treatment and healing involve processing trauma-related memories and feelings, discharging pent-up "fight-or-flight" energy, learning how to regulate intense emotions, and rebuilding the ability to trust other people.

Chapter 10

Rewiring the Brain

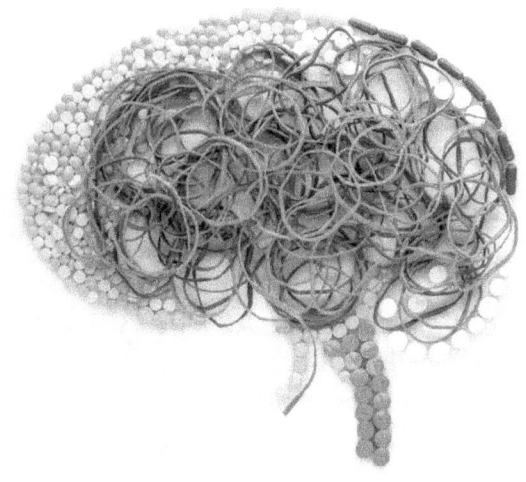

Figure 18

The Process

Recovery, like salvation, is a restorative process to return the individual to a superior pre-injury state. Trauma healing and recovery are processes affected by the optimization of brain function, cultural norms, codes, and health beliefs.

There is a war going in the realm of the spirit. The battle is over your body, soul, and spirit. If you are a believer, your spirit has been redeemed by the blood of the Lamb. Your soul is being redeemed through the renewing of your mind. Your body will be redeemed again when Jesus returns.

The Triune Mind

A brain is a goal-achieving machine. The mind, body, and spirit are crafted for continual communication with God. The brain is comprised of three parts (cerebrum, cerebellum, and brain stem), similar to the triune nature of God as Father, Son, and Holy Spirit, a threefold cord that is not easily broken (Eccl. 4:12).

Elohim (God) said in His Word, "Thou wilt keep him in perfect peace, whose mind is stayed on thee: because he trusteth in thee" (Isa. 26:3).

Words Are Energy

Each time we learn, think, or experience life, we create new neural pathways which serve to connect relatively distant areas in our brain.[1] Words cannot exist without context.

Every word released into the atmosphere consists of molecules that contain energy released into open space.

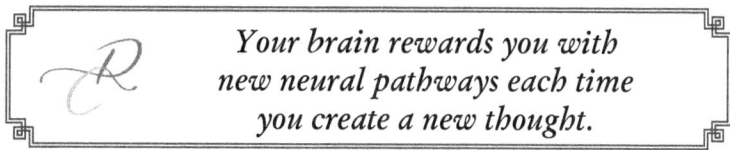

Your brain rewards you with new neural pathways each time you create a new thought.

Re-Route Your Thoughts

You can consciously decide to hack your brain and reroute your thoughts to be assessed at a higher level of thinking. One way to change repetitive negative thought processes is to disallow the mental picture that is counterfeiting as true.

Over time you will establish a new mental map. (A mental map is a first-person perception of one's own world.) Your new mental map will become automatic over time. When these new and more efficient thoughts are superimposed over old, disabling ideas, new neural pathways are created.

Creating New Space for New Thoughts

New neural pathways create open space for replacement thoughts. As you take authority over your thoughts based on the Word of God, new spurts of energy will begin to stream throughout the brain, creating new mental maps—new neural pathways and ways of thinking. Research evidence suggests that the basal ganglia cells are trained to choose behaviors that have been rewarding in the past.

The basal ganglia remember the trigger that causes a habit to be repeated. Each time you establish a new neural pathway, the basal ganglia reward your brain![2]

You are rewarded by your brain [with new neural pathways] for each new thought your mind creates. You can exchange the rewards for feelings of guilt and shame for the rewards of new healthy thoughts of peace and joy!

Habits

Habits are the brain's way of helping us simultaneously memorize and repeat the things we regularly do.

The basal ganglia, located within the limbic system, is responsible for habit formation. Habits are sequences of actions that are learned progressively and are more often performed unconsciously.[3]

Psychology research, published in the *European Journal of Social Psychology*, seems to indicate that it takes around sixty-six days to truly ingrain a new habit into your brain.[4]

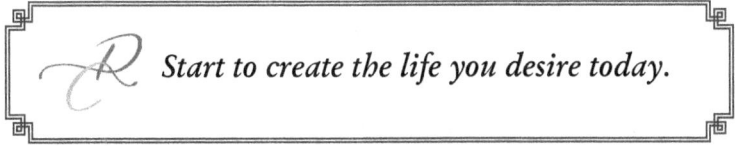
Start to create the life you desire today.

Creating A New Lifestyle

It has generally been accepted that habits are formed between twenty-one to thirty days. Habits are crucial for energy efficiency for the brain. One has to have memorable goals for them to stick. Establishing a goal as a mindset and implementing within a hierarchical order will establish a habit. As mentioned, visualization is critical; it helps to prime the brain.

(Building on my spiritual mother, Dr. Cindy Trimm) Mantra: what you do consistently for thirty days can become a habit. Whatever you do for sixty days consistently can become a practice. After sixty-six days of continuous activity, that habit is going to be as much of a pattern as ever. Whatever you do consistently and consecutively for ninety days can become a lifestyle. In other words, after ninety days, the action becomes automatic.

Start to create the life you desire today. You are eighty-nine days away from making it an automatic reality!

Neuroplasticity

The more we purposefully think differently, the easier it becomes. Eventually, that becomes the brain's unique way of automatically thinking. The brain plasticity, also called neuroplasticity, is behind how habits are formed.[5] Research on brain plasticity and other neuroscientific discoveries have shown that we can increase our neural growth by the actions we take and that connectivity between neurons can change with experiences.[6] The brain's physical composition can alter in response to needs and skill. The cells in your body react to everything that your mind says, which means that if you change the way you look at things, the things you look at will change.

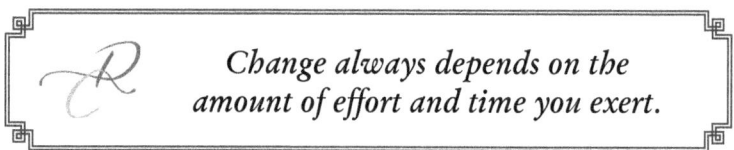

Change always depends on the amount of effort and time you exert.

REGULATIONS OF INTENSE EMOTIONS

The first step in rewiring your brain is to learn how to regulate intense emotions. Once emotions are controlled, you can rebuild the ability to trust the Word of God and the people God has assigned to you.

ACTIVATE NEW NEURAL PATHWAYS

According to Andrew Newberg, a pioneer in the field of neuro-theology (also known as spiritual neuroscience), practices that involve concentrating on something over and over again, either through prayer or a mantra-based meditation, tend to activate the frontal lobes, the areas chiefly responsible for directing attention, modulating behavior, and expressing language.[7]

Change always depends on the amount of effort and time you exert. Use your mind to create new habits through practice or repeated actions.

Donald Hebb's foundational stance forms the basis for the concept of neuroplasticity, which is the ability of the brain to rewire itself. According to Hebb, "As the mind changes, the brain changes.... Neurons that are wired together are fired together," and consequently, the neurons associated with a particular activity function together and form a neural pathway.[8]

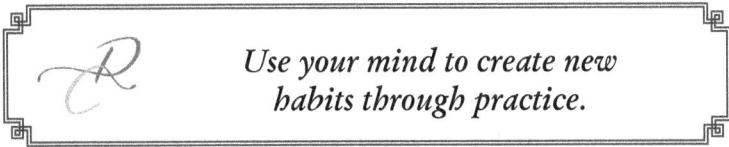

Use your mind to create new habits through practice.

With consistent practice and training, you can rewire the circuitry of the brain to activate new neural pathways according to the habit you want to create. When pathways are not used, they weaken and wear off in time, making room for new neural pathways to form. This is why it is easier to form a new habit than maintain an old one.[9]

ALIGN TO ACTIVATE ALL FRONTS

However, activating one pathway alone is not enough to successfully rewire your brain. New pathways are charted when you repeatedly align your beliefs, feelings, vision, and actions. Then you will experience lasting changes in your brain when those thoughts are in alignment with the Word of God. Mapping new neural pathways will dislodge and evict the spirit of trauma from your body (temple). The Word of God reveals that "whatsoever a man thinks in his heart, so is he" (Prov. 23:7).

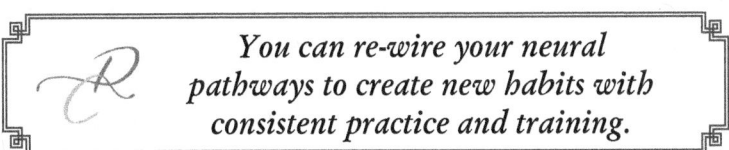

You can re-wire your neural pathways to create new habits with consistent practice and training.

WRITE NEW VISIONS

With the right strategy and focus, you can do all things through Jesus Christ who strengthens you each day. It is possible for you to use your brain to create new habits.

A goal is not a goal unless it is written. Start by writing and create new memories of victory. Yes, there will be distractions along the way. You might relapse into familiar patterns right at the brink of succeeding.

Be mindful that a relapse is not an indication of failure but, rather, the enemy's resistance to the process. How you apply the Word of God will determine how you deal with demonic chatter. How fast you get back up will determine the results.

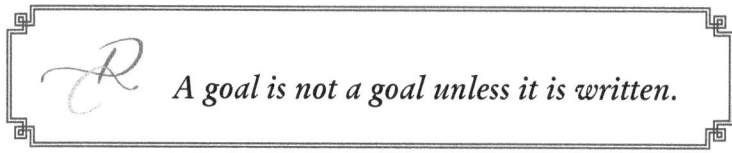

A goal is not a goal unless it is written.

The Trauma of Change System Model

STRATEGIES TO REWIRE THE BRAIN WITH THE WORD OF GOD

1. **Trust in the Word and the promises of God.** Realize that your circumstances have nothing to do with what God has promised you. "Let this mind be in you which was also in Christ Jesus" (Phil. 2:5–11).

Trust is part of your brain's default setting. The anterior cingulate cortex (ACC) is the accountant of the brain, organized to assess reward/risk-based decision making. The ACC is embedded in the prefrontal cortex (PFC). If the actions and beliefs of an individual are not in alignment, it will trigger an alarm to the amygdala. When there is a breach of trust, the brain's conflict detector, the ACC, activates the amygdala. Trust and fear are inversely related. Anxiety activates the amygdala. Trust decreases activation of the amygdala. Trust frees up the brain for other activities like creativity and planning and decision making.

2. **Make a quality decision to adopt new and more effective ways to think, feel, and speak to old, disabling beliefs, triggers, and thoughts.** Meditate on Romans 12:2: "Be not conformed to the world but be transformed by the renewing of your mind." You must be intentional because God is intentional.

3. **Write the thoughts that you want to become part of your mental map.** Create a script for each day. The act of writing stimulates the limbic system's emotional processing, creativity, and insights. Brain science shows that making decisions reduces worry and anxiety and helps you solve problems. Making decisions includes creating intentions and setting goals. Taking action on all three are part of the same neural circuitry and engage the prefrontal cortex in a positive way, reducing worry and anxiety.

4. Give yourself permission to rewrite positive narratives and embrace new positive emotions. An emotion is not a thought. Writing deepens neural pathways for learning.

> "And the Lord answered me, and said, write the vision, and make it plain upon tables, that he may run that readeth it" (Hab. 2:2).

An emotion is a reaction to a positive or negative thought. Human emotions can be viewed as the fuel that drives the car. You can't arrive at your point of destiny on an empty fuel tank. Without an authentic emotion, a thought sits in neutral like a car without gas. Conscious and critical thinking will help you to mentally shift and increase the flow of brain connectivity from the left and right brain, preventing it from being high jacked by the amygdala. The amygdala is wired to detect the threat and how we make decisions, form memories, and encode negative memory into the hippocampus.

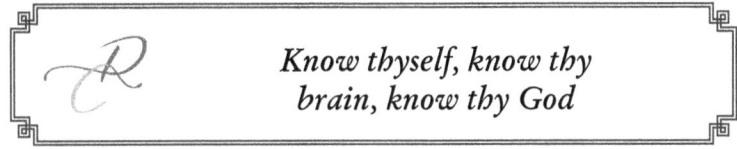

Know thyself, know thy brain, know thy God

5. Give yourself permission to engage in positive thoughts. Gratitude and forgiveness coordinate thoughts and emotions. Gratitude is a constant state of mental appreciation. The benefits of gratitude start with the dopamine system because feeling grateful activates the brain stem region that produces dopamine. Gratitude involves the cerebellum, the emotional brain, the temporal lobe. Gratitude affects your brain at the biological level and boosts the neurotransmitter dopamine. Be intentional in forgiving those who abused and hurt you. In prayer tell God how grateful you are for His presence, favor, and the ability to forgive as He forgives you.

6. Visualize your destination. You must see yourself where you want to be before you arrive there. See yourself as delivered, victorious, and healed from the spirit of trauma. The process of visualization primes the brain. You can use visualization to create the emotions you want to experience. The stronger the feelings are, the stronger the mental map will be.

When you visualize your intentions, your brain can't tell the difference between what is real or imagined. As you mentally rehearse new affirmations and habits, you strengthen your ability to create them in your life and open portals in your right brain

> For as he thinks in his heart, so is he. (Prov 23:7 NKJV)

7. **Speak only the truth of God's Word.** You are a speaking spirit. Your words matter. Words lack meaning without context. Myles Munroe said, "If the context is wrong, the conclusion is also wrong." Your words have to line up with the Word of God to effect change in yourself and your life. "Study to shew thyself approved unto God, a workman that needeth not to be ashamed, rightly dividing the word of truth" (2 Tim. 2:15). Study and meditate on Scriptures about the change you want to create.

As you align your confession with the Word of God, you will overcome. Our words have the power to destroy and the power to build up (Prov. 12:6). The writer of Proverbs tells us, "The tongue has the power of life and death, and those who love it will eat its fruit" (Prov. 18:21 NIV).

Just as God has come for our words, satan comes for your words as well. Anytime you open your mouth you are on trial; words create worlds.

> "For by thy words thou shalt be justified, and by thy words,
> thou shalt be condemned" (Matt. 12:37).

8. **Practice the thoughts you want to dominate your waking day and dreams.** New ideas and experiences create new neural pathways, thought processes, and mental associations. Your mind is renewed as you establish new patterns and practices.

Practice thinking, feeling, visualizing, and acting in alignment with your desired intentions to remove old behaviors and thoughts. When you do this, you give notice to demonic squatters that their time is up by commanding them in the name of Jesus to leave and never return. Repeating new and purposeful actions will become an ingrained and habitual thought process. Be ye transformed by the renewing of your mind.

> "And be not conformed to this world: but be ye transformed
> by the renewing of your mind, that ye may prove what is
> good, and acceptable, and perfect, will of God" (Rom. 12:2).

9. **Declare God's Word to override your past.** Superimpose the truth of what God says about you over the painful, old negative memories.

Change requires practicing a new habit. Continually repeat what the Word of God says until it becomes a part of you. Tap into your heavenly language by praying in the Spirit (in tongues; satan cannot discern what you are saying to God as you pray in supernatural tongues). Praying in the Spirit allows the Word of God to have predominance in your mind. As you declare God's Word over you, it will become true to you.

> "It is the spirit that quickeneth; the flesh profiteth nothing: the words that I speak unto you, they are spirit, and they are life." (John 6:63)

10. As you meditate and speak the Word of God, allow your heart to release and disallow emotions of anxiety, pain, shame, fear, and guilt. It won't be enough to read and recite the Word of God if you don't believe what it says in your life. Introduce yourself to the new experience of healing and deliverance and the new feelings of peace, confidence, hope, and love.

David: A Biblical Example of Rewiring Your Brain in Faith

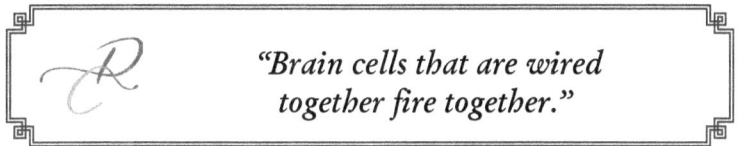

"Brain cells that are wired together fire together."

King David is a perfect example of how you can rewire your brain in faith. The Word of God refers to King David as a man after God's own heart (Acts 13:22).

David experienced childhood abandonment, being rejected by his father. He then suffered persecution and betrayal trauma from King Saul. Furthermore, King David was betrayed by his son Absalom. King David faced one-step transmission trauma when his son Amnon became obsessed with Tamar, his half-sister, and raped her. Moreover, he lost the child conceived as a result of the sin he committed with Bathsheba.

Although David experienced multiple severe traumas, he stood on the Word of God. David practiced narrative memory as evidenced by his writing much of the book of Psalms. Many of the psalms exemplified his faith in God and released his emotions.

> I waited patiently for the Lord, and He inclined to me and heard my cry. He brought me up out of the pit of destruction,

out of the miry clay, and He set my feet on a rock making my footsteps firm. He put a new song in my mouth, a song of praise to our God; many will see and fear and will trust in the Lord." (Ps. 40:1–3 NASB)

If the Lord had not been my help, my soul would soon have dwelt in the abode of silence. If I should say, "My foot has slipped," Your loving kindness, O Lord, will hold me up. When my anxious thoughts multiply within me, your consolations delight my soul. (Ps. 94:17–19 NASB)

Chapter 11

The Altar

The altar is the place where we meet God in worship and position ourselves to experience deliverance.

Steps of Faith

As we physically move our bodies to come to the altar, we move spiritually to meet God in faith. The physical act of coming to the altar is an outward expression of our faith that God's healing and deliverance will meet us there.

Commanded to Come Boldly

We are commanded to come to the throne of grace or the altar of God, especially when we are in trouble and distress. The Word of God tells us in Hebrews 4:16 (NKJV) to "come boldly to the throne of grace, that we may obtain mercy and find grace to help in time of need." When David was in distress, he prayed at "the altar of his soul," saying:

> Be merciful to me, Lord, for I am in distress;
>   my eyes grow weak with sorrow,
>   my soul and body with grief.
> My life is consumed by anguish
>   and my years by groaning;
> my strength fails because of my affliction,
>   and my bones grow weak.
> But I trust in you, Lord;
>   I say, "You are my God."
> My times are in your hands;
>   deliver me from the hands of my enemies,
>   from those who pursue me.
> Let your face shine on your servant;
>   save me in your unfailing love. (Psalm 31:9–10, 14–16 NIV)

LIVING SACRIFICES

As we obey God's commands, we open space for spiritual transformation by presenting our bodies to God. We present our "bodies a living sacrifice, holy, acceptable to God, which is [our] reasonable service" (Rom. 12:1).

ABRAHAM AT THE ALTAR

You may remember the story of Abraham. He and his wife, Sarah, had a son when they were well advanced in years. This child was the fulfillment of a promise that took twenty-five years to manifest. However, when Isaac was still young, God tested Abraham. He told him, "Take your son, your only son, whom you love—Isaac—and go to the region of Moriah. Sacrifice him there as a burn to offering on a mountain I will show you (Gen. 22:2 NIV).

I cannot imagine what must have been going through Abraham's mind. Abraham loved Isaac, and as traumatic as the thought of killing him was, he remembered when the Lord appeared to him at the age of ninety-nine and said, "I am God All-Powerful. If you obey me and always do right, I will keep my solemn promise to you and give you more descendants than can be counted" (Gen. 17:1–2 CEV).

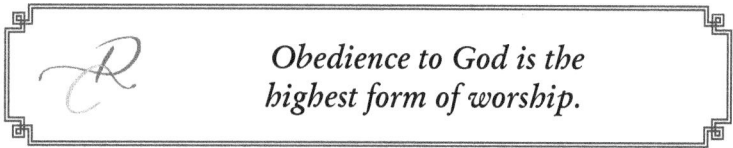

Obedience to God is the highest form of worship.

Abraham obediently presented Isaac on Mount Moriah as a sacrificial offering to God—the ultimate demonstration of faith. Fortunately, this was only a test. God told Abraham to stop just as he was raising the knife to kill his son, and the Lord provided a ram to serve as the sacrifice. After this encounter, Abraham called God *Jehovah Jireh*, or "the Lord who provides." Obedience to God is the highest form of worship.

At the altar, through this difficult situation, God revealed Himself to Abraham in a new way and brought him closer to Himself. God still does the same thing today. He uses difficult conditions to draw His people to Himself. Moreover, He intends that something is to be "altered" when we come to the altar.

The Trauma of Change System Model: Recovery Processing Stage

In concert with the Trauma of Change System Model philosophy, we embrace the concept that *recovery* is a process of spiritual development and growth that involves the whole person. Recovery is an evolving process beginning with a readiness to examine and discard self-defeating beliefs and behaviors. The TOC System Model foundational concept is:

Recovery is a God-directed self-help process, influenced by genuine desire to achieve a settled state of deliverance and healing.

Figure 18

Following the stage processing steps to facilitate recovery outlined in the Trauma of Change System Model, combined with the steps described on how to rewire the brain, will have a significant impact on healing trauma wounds and bruises.

RESET: Recovery Process Stage 1

The Reset stage of recovery involves a mindset shift to restore individuals back to their pre-trauma state. This is a phase of challenging self-doubt and disabling beliefs emanating from the spirit of trauma.

DISCIPLINE: Recovery Process Stage 2

The Discipline stage consists of advancing the stage-processing techniques of deliverance and healing through change and transformation. Fasting is recommended and requires discipline, which develops a resilient mind and produces ketones as an alternative fuel source for the brain.

EMBRACE: Recovery Process Stage 3

The Embrace stage involves embracing the Six Psychological Tools of Recovery: forgiveness, humility, responsibility, dedication, truthfulness, and honesty. Knowing your identity, position, purpose, and significance in Christ Jesus is essential for sealing the deliverance process. This phase is marked by your ability to define and understand your purpose and destiny according to the will of God.

STABILITY: Recovery Process Stage 4

The Stability stage involves new stability in the face of trauma. This stage marks a period of significant growth as evidenced by continuous progress in applying the Six Psychological Tools of Recovery.

Forgiveness heals emotional wounds and changes the brain. It involves the reappraisal process and recruits several regions within the prefrontal lobes and is involved with empathy and emotional regulation.

Demonstrating **gratitude** will catapult you into a constant state of mental appreciation. Gratitude increases our brain's dopamine levels, affecting it at a biological level, and boosts the production of the neurotransmitter's serotonin in the anterior singular. Gratitude is a constant state of mental appreciation and coordinate thoughts and emotions. Gratitude forces you to focus on the positive aspect of your life.[1]

CHAPTER 12

The Final Word

If you have experienced a trauma that has now become a stronghold in your life, I recommend you pray and seek a professionally trained, faith-based, trauma-informed therapist or a neuro-coach who will empower you to create new neural pathways. Through competent talk therapy, a professionally trained, qualified trauma specialist can help you rewrite old memories in a safe space and guide you towards healing.

A Word to Practitioners

The practitioner working with a survivor of trauma must be mindful of how to activate deliverance and healing through the use of biblio-neuro-technologies to set the captive free, eradicate the memory of the trauma, and facilitate recovery. Many people have experienced trauma. Moreover, many Christians in the church still wrestle with remnants of traumatic memories. Satan has used trauma to infiltrate their minds with shame and guilt about their past and present and prevent them from fully manifesting the glory of God.

A Word to Trauma Conquerors

If you think of yourself as a victim, victimization will be dominant in your life. If you think of yourself as a more than a conqueror, victory belongs to you, and you will rise up victorious each day. Begin to rewire your brain and renew your mind every day. Invite the Holy Spirit to dominate your thoughts, then review the prayers in this book and pray until you see results.

A Word to the Helpers

Don't merely limit the knowledge gained from this book for application to your own life. Use what you've learned to help others who have also experienced severe hurt in the past. This will ensure that the cycle of healing continues, and others are finally able to break free of their pain.

We often share painful experiences and trauma wounds. Let's replace the old cycles of shared hurt and create new cycles of shared healing. Be the hands and feet of Christ by sharing this book with those who need healing. Their lives, too, will be transformed.

A Word to Clergy

For those in ministry who may have never experienced significant trauma, know that you are blessed with the assignment to minister to those whose experiences compromise their deliverance. Practice patience with those bruised souls in the beginning stages of deliverance.

Intercede compassionately on their behalf as they work to recognize their own strength and the strength of God.

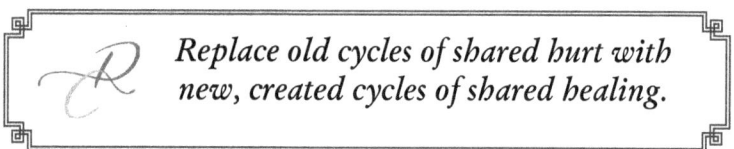

Replace old cycles of shared hurt with new, created cycles of shared healing.

Healing must occur for people to be free of all that has held a person bound in the past—to proclaim God's glory. It is because of this need that I have written this book. I hope it blesses those who have gone through severe, gut-wrenching traumas in their lives. I pray God will heal and meet the individual needs of those who are held in bondage by the spirit of trauma. It is my joy to see people living in victory over life challenges. I sincerely hope this book fulfills this great yearning of my heart.

Appendix 1

ACE Screening

Figure 19

Adverse Childhood Experience (ACE) Questionnaire

To determine your ACE score, complete the following questions.

Before your eighteenth birthday:

1. Did a parent or other adult in the household often or very often swear at you, insult you, put you down, humiliate you, or act in a way that made you afraid that you might be physically hurt?

    If yes, enter 1 _____

2. Did a parent or other adult in the household often or very often push, grab, slap, or throw something at you or ever hit you so hard that you had marks or were injured?

Apendix 1

If yes, enter 1 _____

3. Did an adult or person at least five years older than you ever touch or fondle you or have you touch their body in a sexual way or attempt or actually have oral, anal, or vaginal intercourse with you?

   If yes, enter 1 _____

4. Did you often or very often feel that no one in your family loved you or thought you were important or special, or that your family didn't look out for one another, feel close to one another, or support one another?

   If yes, enter 1 _____

5. Did you often or very often feel that you didn't have enough to eat, had to wear dirty clothes, or had no one to protect you, or were your parents too drunk or high to take care of you or take you to the doctor if you needed it?

   If yes, enter 1 _____

6. Were your parents ever separated or divorced?

   If yes, enter 1 _____

7. Was your mother or stepmother often or very often pushed, grabbed, slapped, or had something thrown at her? Or was she sometimes, often, or very often kicked, bitten, hit with a fist, or hit with something hard? Or was she ever repeatedly hit over at least a few minutes or threatened with a gun or knife?

   If yes, enter 1 _____

8. Did you live with anyone who was a problem drinker or alcoholic or who used street drugs?

   If yes, enter 1 _____

9. Was a household member depressed or mentally ill, or did a household member attempt suicide?

   If yes, enter 1 _____

10. Did a household member go to prison?

   If yes, enter 1 _____

Now add up your "yes" answers: _____ This is your ACE score.

At least 70 percent of our population has an ACE score of at least one. It does not provide a formal diagnosis, but if your score is high, and you're having a rough time in life—related to those adverse experiences—you might want to seek professional help. As your ACE score increases, so do the risk of disease and social and emotional problems.

Remember, the ACE test, as with any self-administered study, should only be used as a guideline.

APPENDIX 2

ACE Screening Score Results

A Score of 0: alcoholism: 3%; chronic depression: 18% (women), 10% (men) liver disease: 5% risk of perpetrating domestic violence: 3% smoking as an adult: 7% being raped later in life: 5% attempting suicide: <2%.

A score of 1: alcoholism: 6%; chronic depression: 22% (women), 20% (men); liver disease: 6%; risk of perpetrating domestic violence: 3%; smoking as an adult: 7%; being raped later in life: 10%; attempting suicide: 3%

A score of 2: alcoholism: 10%; chronic depression: 35% (women), 25% (men); liver disease: 8%; risk of perpetrating domestic violence: 4%; smoking as an adult: 9%; being raped later in life: 16%; attempting suicide: 5%

A score of 3: alcoholism: 11%; chronic depression: 35% (women), 30% (men); liver disease: 10%; risk of perpetrating domestic violence: 7%; smoking as an adult: 11%; being raped later in life: 18%; attempting suicide: 11%

A score of 4 or higher: alcoholism: 16%; chronic depression: 58% (women), 35% (men); liver disease: 11%; risk of perpetrating domestic violence: 6%; smoking as an adult: 13%; being raped later in life: 32%; attempting suicide: 18%

APPENDIX 3

Prayer of Petition by Evangelist Renée D. Charles

The following prayer of deliverance may be used to petition the Lord as you navigate the process of healing, delivery, and recovery.

Father, at your command I arose for no other purpose than to worship and praise You. You alone are God. Beside Thee, there is no other.

Almighty and sovereign God, hear this prayer as I minister to You with thanksgiving and gratitude. Thank You for the breath of life. I could not see, walk, feel, or even think if You did not allow it. Father, in You, do I live, move, and have my being. I acknowledge You as Lord, and I bow my knee unto Thee.

I have endured suffering and deep wounds and bruises to my soul. I stand at the precipice of intercession for myself (and for others who suffer as I have). In the spirit of Abraham, I ask You to deliver us from every stronghold inhibiting our praise to You. Father, You are sovereign and can exact favor as You please on the just and the unjust.

Father, You promised that You would be our shield and buckler. You said in Your Word that no good thing would You withhold from those who walk uprightly. Father, You said we are joint heirs with Your Son, Jesus, and that You put all things under His feet and gave Him to be head over all things to the church. Heal us from the memory of demonic calamity, intimidation, and self-destruction.

Father, in the name of Jesus I curse at the root the memory of sexual abuse and all forms of abandonment, betrayal, and rejection. In Jesus's name, I come against demonic surveillance looking for a crack in my body temple. I disallow and nullify the growth of cancerous impressions hidden in the temple of those who trust and believe Your Word concerning healing and deliverance. I forbid the replay and projection of traumatic events presented as a reenactment of the trauma endured. I prohibit self-doubt and low self-esteem to replicate any further, not only in this present time but also in the spiritual DNA of future generations.

In the name of Jesus, I take jurisdictional authority at the level of my matron to disrupt and dismantle the plans and purposes of the enemy. I exalt the plans and purposes that You have for my ministry, my family, my businesses, my churches, and my home.

Father, in the name of Jesus, please heal everyone who has been abandoned, betrayed, and abused as Your Son was.

Father, superimpose Your will over the will of evil men and any demonic squatters that attempt to reside in our bodies, minds, and souls.

Father, I am afflicted and bruised. I expect You to answer this prayer because of who You are and by Your divine systems of the protocol. I believe in miracles. I decree that You are a faithful and a just God. You are a great God. You are an awesome God. You alone can handle these diseases and tragedies.

God, I don't know how You are going to do it. I know that Your divine plans will prevail. I present my body as a living sacrifice, holy and acceptable unto You as my reasonable service. Father, in the name of Jesus, let this prayer be a sweet smell in Your nostrils.

Amen.

Appendix 4

Deliverance Declaration

These declarations are written in full on Archbishop Duncan Williams's website, http://www.ggcogic.org/uploads/34-StrategicPrayerPoints2018.pdf. Open the webpage and repeat the declarations out loud. *Pray all points with the understanding that they are claimed through the blood of Jesus and authority is taken in the name of Jesus!*

The declarations cover the following aspects:

1. Confession and forgiveness
2. Satanic covenants, agreements, exchanges, vows, or transactions made by your descendants
3. All the works of satan
4. All satanic projections on your life
5. Your position in heavenly places
6. The timing of your written destiny
7. Divine solutions
8. Acts of injustice and harassment
9. God's rule in your favor
10. Overcoming the enemy
11. Binding the strong man
12. The advancement and takeover of satan's territory
13. The destruction and removal of every form of evil in the church
14. The transfer of wealth and power into the kingdom
15. The uncovering of false prophets
16. Interference in opportunities
17. Denying the enemy access

18. Releasing the blessings of the Lord
19. Denying demonic spirits access
20. The washing of the blood of Jesus
21. Divine order
22. Individual and corporate worship
23. Divine protection
24. Favor for your children
25. Long life and health
26. Enlargement of the territory of the church
27. A renewed spirit of holiness, unity, and boldness
28. Distraction
29. Revoking of every death wish
30. Overthrow and reversal of all satanic sanctions

APPENDIX 5

How to Close All Doors to Satan

The kingdom of God and the kingdom of satan generally operate by legal rights or open doorways. Unless we open the door of our lives to God, He can't come into our lives to be our personal Savior, healer, and deliverer. That is why Jesus said in Revelation 3:20, "Behold, I stand at the door and knock: if any man hear my voice and open the door, I will come in to him, and will sup with him, and he with me."

If you don't allow Him in, He won't come in. Have you invited Jesus to be your Savior, healer, and deliverer? If you haven't, please open the door of your life to Him now.

In the same way, the devil generally can't come into your life except the door be opened to him. Unlike God, who only comes in by your personal prayer of invitation, satan can enter many open doors. Some of those "doors" are through thoughts and actions most people think are harmless. Certain problems and demonic attacks we experience are a direct result of doors that have been opened to satan unknowingly.

Unless you close those doors, satan has legal right to operate in your life and to steal, kill, and destroy any blessing in your life.

Demonic Doorstops

A doorstop is a small plastic, rubber, or metal object placed at the edge of a doorframe to prevent full closure. Until the doorstop is removed, the door will remain open. The first step to take in receiving deliverance from all demonic attacks and problems is making sure all doors are closed to satan.

How can you close doors unless you know what has opened the door to the enemy in your life? Here is a list of demonic doorstops that open the door to the devil.

1. **A family background in the occult or false religions.**

> **Exodus 20:1–5.** Examples of cults and false religions include Rosicrucian, Masons, Mormonism, Jehovah's Witness, palm reading, psychics, tarot card reading, and bush bath.

Whenever you visit the psychic, root workers, or spiritual readers, you open the door of your life to their god, satan. Many people are deceived because the things these psychics or "readers" tell them about themselves are true or come true. They submit to the commands or advice of these people because they think they possess gifts from God. What they don't know is that the devil, too, can see. These psychics work hand in hand with familiar or demonic spirits and get information about people from the spirits. Just because someone is able to perform signs and wonders does not mean they are doing it through the power of God.

There are many spiritual or "white garment" churches around the city. Some of them worship angels or African deities like Sango, Orisha, Yemoja, or Ogun. If you've involved yourself with these people and their practices, you've opened your life to demonic attacks and need deliverance.

Every time you go to the devil for protection or anything else, he gives you his demonic spirits, which manifest themselves in your life as bad luck, curses, night visitors, and so on. You must repent of your worship of false gods and renounce them.

2. **Negative prenatal influences**, such as visiting a witch doctor before or while pregnant or thoughts of having an abortion.

3. **Pressures in early childhood,** such as sexual abuse and childhood rivalry.

4. **Emotional shock or sustained emotional pressure.** For example, witnessing a murder or being in a burning building.

5. **Sinful acts or habits.** Because of their sin, Ananias and Sapphira opened themselves to be filled with spirits of covetousness, lying, and deceit (Acts 5:3; John 5:14).

6. **Perverse laying on of hands.** Just as the Holy Spirit can be imparted through the laying on of hands (Acts 19:6), demonic spirits can be transferred through the laying on of hands (transference of spirits). You can't allow just anybody to lay hands on you. It does not matter what their title or position is. You need to test all spirits and make sure they are of God before you allow them to lay hands on you. It is very dangerous to go from church to church in search of help. Many people have become possessed, and their problems have worsened because they visited a pastor with "another spirit" not of God. Be careful.

7. **Ancestral inheritance.** Sometimes the source of your problem is not you. Sometimes it is your ancestors who made a covenant with satan years ago. Now you are suffering from the results of the agreement.

Just as a person can inherit diabetes from their family genes, a person can inherit curses, hindrances, and blockages from their family line. The Bible makes it clear that God visits the iniquities of the father upon the children to the third and fourth generation (Ex. 20:5). That means you may be suffering from the sins and evil work that your ancestors committed 160 years ago. These acts become destiny changes in your life. The devil does not give anything without demanding a great price in return. Like Daniel and Jeremiah (Dan. 9:16; Jer. 14:20), confess the sins of your ancestors and ask for forgiveness on their behalf so that the curses may be lifted. If they have signed any contract with the devil, break, destroy, and renounce those covenants immediately.

8. **Demonic contact**, such as playing with Ouija board.

9. **Cultural dance, rituals, and pagan festivals and artwork.** Some cultural and ritual events allow the worship of deities and idols. We view these rituals as being merely cultural and see little to no harm in participating in them. Allowing children to dress for Halloween and other festivals opens demonic spiritual doors.

10. **Unforgiveness.** The failure to forgive caused the unjust

steward to be turned over to the "tormentors" (Matt. 18:1). Demon spirits are tormentors.

11. **Charms.** "Good luck" charms or those that are worn for protection are demonic. Only God can protect people. Any other source of protection is demonic and invites demons and curses into your life.

12. **Haunted places.** The name alone should make you beware. Locations that claim to be haunted are often ancestral sacrificial grounds. They are sites dedicated to ruling spirits that bring curses.

13. **Music, movies, and books.** There is a demonic agenda to demonize people, especially children. Some of the movies and music that youths listen to are demonic. These mediums are used subtly to introduce children to witchcraft and magic. Books like Harry Porter make it seem alright to dabble in magic and witchcraft.

This article was extracted from Pastor K. Femi's Deliverance Today Bulletin.

About the Author

Dr. Renée Charles is a thought-leader consultant, speaker, author, trainer, and independent executive coach-consultant with the John Maxwell and IPEC Core Energy Teams. Dr. Charles holds an earned doctorate (Ph.D.) and possesses competencies as a professional coach with certifications in emotional intelligence, cultural intelligence, neuro-coaching, core energy leadership, cultural competence leadership training, faith-based counselor training, and ecumenical coaching.

Dr. Charles is a cultural competence leadership fellow and one of the leading experts on minority health and racial and ethnic health disparities. She is a voice for those who are at the beginning stages of recognizing their strength and devotes her professional life to increasing the social, emotional, and cultural intelligence of patients, clients, and the professional community at large about racial-ethnic health disparities. Dr. Charles's global reach is facilitating excellence in personal, executive, and corporate leadership by adding value to leaders who will also add value to others. Her career has spanned clinical practice, program administration, clinical research, professional training, and mentoring.

Dr. Charles is the founder of the Center for Rapid Recovery (CRR) in Hempstead, New York, which carved out a mission to improve access to culturally and linguistically competent care and reduce the prevalence of racial and ethnic disparities in healthcare. She is also a licensed evangelist and serves on the ministerial board at her local church, Zion Cathedral, and within Third Ecclesiastical Jurisdiction of Eastern New York under the leadership of Senior Pastor Bishop Frank A. White, National Secretary of Finance of COGIC and Jurisdictional Bishop of the Third Ecclesiastical Jurisdiction of Eastern New York (ENY).

Dr. Charles provides leadership within Zion Cathedral and the Third Ecclesiastical Jurisdiction (ENY) and local church as the president of the counseling department and serves on the examination and ordination

Endnotes

Author's Note

1. Debbie Hampton, "How Your Mind Shapes Your Brain," The Best Brain Possible, February 14, 2016, www.thebestbrainpossible.com/how-your-mind-shapes-your-brain.

Prologue

1. Hampton, "How Your Mind Shapes Your Brain."

2. Ananya Mandal, MD, "Human Brain Structure," News Medical Life Science, accessed February 28, 2019, https://www.news-medical.net/health/Human-Brain-Structure.aspx.

3. Debbie Hampton, "What's the Difference Between Feelings and Emotions?" The Best Brain Possible, accessed February 25, 2019, https://www.thebestbrainpossible.com/whats-the-difference-between-feelings-and-emotions.

4. Karl Perera, "Self Concept and Self Esteem," More-Selfesteem.com, accessed February 28, 2019, https://www.more-selfesteem.com/self_concept.htm.

5. Marty, "Trauma Memories are sensory fragments," *C PTSD—A Way Out* (blog), January 10, 2018, https://www.ptsdawayout.com/2018/01/10/trauma-memories-are-sensory-fragments/.

6. Arjun Walia, "Quantum Experiment Shows How 'Time' Doesn't Exist As We Think It Does (Mind-Altering)," Collective Evolution, July 2, 2015, https://www.collective-evolution.com/2015/07/20/quantum-experiment-shows-how-time-doesnt-exist-as-we-think-it-does-mind-altering.

7. Witness Lee, "Dealing with Our Inward Parts for the Growth in Life," Living Stream Ministry, Accessed February 28, 2019, https://www.ministrysamples.org/excerpts/THE-SOUL-HAVING-THREE-PARTS.HTML

8. Ibid.

9. *New World Encyclopedia*, s.v. "Ego, superego, and id," accessed February 28, 2019, http://www.newworldencyclopedia.org/p/index.php?title=Ego%2C_superego%2C_and_id.

10. "You Can't Have One without the Other: How Body Systems are Connected," RevereHealth, August 22, 2016, https://reverehealth.com/live-better/how-body-systems-connected.

11. *Merriam-Webster*, s.v. "trauma (*noun*)," accessed February 28, 2019, https://www.merriam-webster.com/dictionary/trauma.

12. SAMHSA-HRSA Center for Integrated Health Solutions, s.v. "Trauma," accessed February 28, 2019, http://www.integration.samhsa.gov/clinical-practice/trauma.

13. "Post Traumatic Stress Disorder Fact Sheet," Sidran Institute, accessed February 28, 2019, https://www.sidran.org/.../post-traumatic-stress-disorder-fact-sheet.

14. "Sexual Violence, Stalking, and Intimate Partner Violence Widespread in the US," Centers for Disease Control and Prevention, December 14, 2011, https://www.cdc.gov/media/releases/2011/p1214_sexual_violence.html.

15 Farahnaz Mohammed, "The Repetition Compulsion: Why Rape Victims Are More Likely To Be Assaulted Again," Girls' Globe, August 4, 2015, https://www.girlsglobe.org/2015/08/04/the-repetition-compulsion-why-rape-victims-are-more-likely-to-be-assaulted-again, emphasis added.

16 Esther Giller, "What Is Psychological Trauma?" Sidran Institute, accessed February 28, 2019, https://www.sidran.org/resources/for-survivors-and-loved-ones/what-is-psychological-trauma.

17 Ibid.

18 "Child Maltreatment 2001: Reports from the States to the National Child Abuse and Neglect Data System," Children's Bureau, Agency for Children and Families, 2003

19 *Teen Support Group Guide: A Guide to Psychoeducational Support Groups for Teen Survivors of Sexual Abuse and Assault* (Olympia, WA: Washington Coalition of Sexual Assault Programs, 2013), 6, http://www.ncdsv.org/images/WCSAP_CircleOfHope-TeenSupportGroup_2013.pdf

20 "Substance Abuse as a Consequence of Sexual Abuse," DARA Thailand, accessed February 28, 2019, https://alcoholrehab.com/drug-addiction/substance-abuse-consequence-sexual-abuse.

21 Paula Domenici, Keith Armstrong, and Suzanne Best, *Courage After Fire for Parents of Service Members* (Oakland, CA: New Harbinger Publications, 2013).

22 Ibid.

23 "Child Abuse Statistics & Facts," Childhelp, accessed February 28, 2019, https://www.childhelp.org/child-abuse-statistics/.

24 "Suicide Statistics," Suicide.org, accessed February 28, 2019, http://www.suicide.org/suicide-statistics.html.

25 "Body-Based Therapies for Stress, Trauma, and PTSD," Yogacalm, accessed February 28, 2019, https://www.yogacalm.org/body-based-therapies-for-trauma-and-ptsd.

Chapter 1

1 Ibrahim Aref Kira, *Taxonomy of Trauma and Trauma Assessment*, June 2011, https://www.myptsd.com/gallery/-pdf/1-88.pdf.

2 "Sanctuary Institute: The Sanctuary Model," Sanctuary Institute, accessed March 11, 2017, http://thesanctuaryinstitute.org/about-us/the-sanctuary-model

3 Bessel A. van der Kolk, MD and Onno van der Hart, Ph.D., "Pierre Janet & the Breakdown of Adaptation in Psychological Trauma," *American Journal of Psychiatry*, 146 (12), December 1989, 1530–40.

4 Jonah Lehrer, "The Forgetting Pill Erases Painful Memories Forever," Wired, February 17, 2012, https://www.wired.com/2012/02/ff-forgettingpill/.

5 Wikipedia, s.v. "Fight-or-flight response," accessed February 28, 2019, https://en.wikipedia.org/wiki/Fight-or-flight_response.

6 Dr. Sandra L. Bloom, "The Sanctuary Model," accessed February 28, 2019, www.

sanctuaryweb.com/Portals/Trauma.pdf

7   Trauma-Informed Care in Behavioral Health Services, (Rockville, MD: Substance Abuse and Mental Health Services Administration, 2014), chap. 3, https://www.ncbi.nlm.nih.gov/books/NBK207191.

8   Genevieve Mary Catherine Pruneau, "Distinctiveness of Avoidance and Numbing in PTSD," (master's thesis, Auburn University, 2008), https://etd.auburn.edu/bitstream/handle/10415/25/Pruneau_Genevieve_10.pdf;sequence=1

9   Theresa Burke, Ph.D., "How Trauma Impacts the Brain," Rachel's Vineyard, accessed February 28, 2019, http://www.rachelsvineyard.org/Downloads/Canada%20Conference%2008/TextOfBrainPP.pdf.

10   Bessel A. van der Kolk, MD, "The Compulsion oo Repeat the Trauma: Re-enactment, Revictimization, and Masochism," Psychiatric Clinics of North America, Volume 12, Number 2, Pages 389–411, June 1989, http://www.traumacenter.org/products/pdf_files/Compulsion_to_Repeat.pdf.

11   Richard P. Fitzgibbons, "The Cognitive and Emotive Uses of Forgiveness in the Treatment of Anger," *Psychotherapy*, Volume 23/Winter 1986/Number 4, priestlyhealing.com/sites/default/files/images/Forgiveness_'86.pdf.

12   R. Charles, "Middle Passage Trauma," (doctoral dissertation conceptual framework proposal, Stony Brook University, 2000), chap. 2: Algorithms, Codes, and Data Files.

Chapter 2

1   Dan Ketchum, "Different Parts of the Computer and Their Function," Techwalla, March 31, 2015, https://www.techwalla.com/articles/different-parts-of-the-computer-and-their-function.

2   "Neuroscience," JoVE, accessed October 22, 2018, https://www.jove.com/science-education-library/5/neuroscience.

3   "Child Development: Development of the Human Brain," ER Services, accessed October 22, 2018, https://courses.lumenlearning.com/atd-hostos-childdevelopment/chapter/development-of-the-human-brain.

4   Regina Bailey, "The Four Cerebral Cortex Lobes of the Brain," ThoughtCo., updated September 5, 2018, https://www.thoughtco.com/cerebral-cortex-lobes-anatomy-373197.

5   Ibid.

6   Wikipedia, s.v. "Limbic system," accessed October 22, 2018, https://en.wikipedia.org/wiki/Limbic_system.

7   NeuroSensory Center of Eastern Pennsylvania, "Dizziness and Balance Disorders," accessed October 22, 2018, http://www.keystonensc.com/downloads/epa-dizziness.pdf.

8   Mayfield Brain & Spine, "Anatomy of the Brain," Mayfield Clinic.com, accessed October 22, 2018, https://d3djccaurgtij4.cloudfront.net/pe-anatomybrain.pdf.

9   "The Amygdala & Emotions," Effective Mind Control, updated October 19, 2015, https://www.effective-mind-control.com/amygdala.html.

10 Mayfield, "Anatomy of the Brain."

11 "Hippocampus," The Brain Made Simple, accessed October 22, 2018, http://brainmadesimple.com/hippocampus.html.

12 Regina Bailey, "Basal Ganglia Function," ThoughtCo., updated October 23, 2018, https://www.thoughtco.com/basal-ganglia-function-4086411.

13 Rhawn Gabriel Joseph, Ph.D., "Cingulate Gyrus," Brainmind.com, accessed October 22, 2018, www.brainmind.com/Cingulate.html.

14 Mayfield, "Anatomy of the Brain."

15 "Cerebellum," Healthline, accessed October 22, 2018, https://www.healthline.com/human-body-maps/cerebellum#1.

16 Encyclopaedia Britannica, s.v. "Midbrain," accessed March 7, 2019, https://www.britannica.com/science/midbrain.

17 Mayfield, "Anatomy of the Brain."

18 Ananya Mandal, MD, "What is the Nervous System?" accessed October 22, 2018, https://www.news-medical.net/health/What-is-the-Nervous-System.aspx.

19 "Difference Between Grey and White Matter," differencebetween.net, accessed October 22, 2018, http://www.differencebetween.net/science/health/difference-between-grey-and-white-matter/.

20 Encyclopedia Britannica, s.v. "Midbrain," accessed October 22, 2018, https://www.britannica.com/science/midbrain.

21 "Medical Definition of Glial cell," MedicineNet, accessed October 22, 2018, https://www.medicinenet.com/script/main/art.asp?articlekey=11382.

22 "Trauma Transference Syndrome," accessed October 22, 2018, www.traumatransferencesyndrome.com.

23 "10 Common Negative Thinking Patterns and How You Can Change Them," The Best Brain Possible with Debbie Hampton, July 22, 2018, https://www.thebestbrainpossible.com/negative-thinking-depression-mind/.

24 Encyclopedia Britannica, s.v. "Midbrain."

25 "What's The Difference Between The Mind And The Brain?" The Best Brain Possible with Debbie Hampton, September 12, 2014, https://www.thebestbrainpossible.com/the-mind-and-the-brain-what-is-the-difference/.

26 "Trauma Transference Syndrome," accessed October 22, 2018, www.traumatransferencesyndrome.com.

27 "What is the limbic system of the brain?" ShareCare, accessed October 22, 2018, https://www.sharecare.com/health/functions-of-the-brain/what-is-limbic-system-brain.

28 Ibid.

29 Christopher Bergland, "Unconscious Memories Hide In the Brain but Can Be Retrieved,"

Psychology Today, August 17, 2015, https://www.psychologytoday.com/us/blog/the-athletes-way/201508/unconscious-memories-hide-in-the-brain-can-be-retrieved.

30   Ibid.

31   Michael Schmid, "Narrative memory and the impact of trauma on individuals with reference to one short sequence from 'Memento,'" Term paper (Munich, 2004), GRIN Verlag, https://www.grin.com/document/66502.

Chapter 3

1   Kathleen Brown Rice, "Examining the Theory of Historical Trauma Among Native Americans," The Professional Counselor, accessed October 22, 2018, http://tpcjournal.nbcc.org/examining-the-theory-of-historical-trauma-among-native-americans/.

2   Ibrahim Aref Kira, *Taxonomy of Trauma and Trauma Assessment*, June 2011, https://www.myptsd.com/gallery/-pdf/1-88.pdf.

3   S. J. Weiss, "Neurobiological alterations associated with traumatic stress. *Perspectives in Psychiatric Care*, 43(3), 114–122. doi:10.1111/j.1744-6163.2007.00120.x.

4   Rice, "Examining the Theory of Historical Trauma Among Native Americans."

5   Ibid.

6   Kira, *Taxonomy of Trauma and Trauma Assessment*.

7   Ibid.

8   Ibid.

9   Ibid.

10   Ibid.

11   Ibid.

12   Dr. Maria YellowHorse-BraveHeart, "Austen's Worldview Through Elizabeth's Eyes Essay," accessed March 8, 2019, https://www.bartleby.com/essay/ Austens-Worldview-Through-Elizabeths-Eyes-F3QP9LYVC.

13   Rice, "Examining the Theory of Historical Trauma Among Native Americans."

14   Ibid.

15   "Born in Slavery: Slave Narratives from the Federal Writers' Project, 1936-1938," Library of Congress, accessed October 22, 2018, http://www.loc.gov/teachers/classroommaterials/connections/narratives-slavery/history.html.

16   Marian F. MacDorman, Ph.D., and T.J. Mathews, MS, "Understanding Racial and Ethnic Disparities in U.S. Infant Mortality Rates," NCHS Data Brief, September 2011, U.S. Department of Health and Human Services, https://www.cdc.gov/nchs/data/databriefs/db74.pdf.

17   "1850 Census: Mortality Statistics of the Seventh Census of the United States, 1850," United States Census Bureau, accessed October 22, 2018, https://www.census.gov/library/

publications/1855/dec/1850b.html.

18   "Unequal Treatment: Confronting Racial and Ethnic Disparities in Health Care," The National Academies of Sciences, Engineering, Medicine, accessed October 22, 2018, http://www.nationalacademies.org/hmd/Reports/2002/Unequal-Treatment-Confronting-Racial-and-Ethnic-Disparities-in-Health-Care.aspx.

19   K. Aurandt, "The Legal Story of the Pennsylvania: A Forward-to-Aft Inspection of a Landmark Admiralty Case." *Journal of Maritime Law and Commerce*, (2014) 45(3), 319.

Chapter 4

1   Sarah Mae Sincero, "Self-Concept Theory," Explorable, accessed October 22, 2018,, https://explorable.com/self-concept-theory.

2   Esther Giller, "What Is Psychological Trauma?" Sidran Institute, accessed October 22, 2018, https://www.sidran.org/resources/for-%20survivors-and-loved-ones/what-is-psychological-trauma/.

3   Ibrahim Aref Kira, *Taxonomy of Trauma and Trauma Assessment*, June 2011, https://www.myptsd.com/gallery/-pdf/1-88.pdf.

4   Wikipedia, s.v. "Self-esteem," accessed October 22, 2018, en.wikipedia.org/wiki/Self-esteem.

5   Kira, *Taxonomy of Trauma and Trauma Assessment*.

6   Eric Berne MD, "Transactional Analysis," EricBerne.com, accessed October 22, 2018, http://www.ericberne.com/transactional-analysis/.

7   Shaun Brookhouse, "Ego States In Transactional Analysis," Hypnotherapy Manchester, accessed October 22, 2018, https://hypnomanchester.co.uk/ego-states-in-transactional-analysis.

8   Ibid.

9   Meltem Tepebaş, "Transactional Analysis Theory: the Basics," Prezi, updated December 23, 2015, https://prezi.com/nv3r8wss7cnr/transactional-analysis-theory-the-basics/.

10 "An Introduction to Ego States," Counselling Connection, accessed October 22, 2018, https://www.counsellingconnection.com/index.php/2009/06/22/an-introduction-to-ego-states.

11 Ibid.

12 Ibid.

13 Ibid.

14 Ibrahim Aref Kira, *Taxonomy of Trauma and Trauma Assessment*.

15 Abdel Aziz Mousa Thabet, "Risk and Protective Factors in Relation to Trauma and Post Traumatic Stress Disorders: A Meta-Analytic Review," EC Psychology and Psychiatry 2.4 (2017): 122–38.

16 Lawrence Robinson, Melinda Smith, MA, and Jeanne Segal, Ph.D., "Emotional and

Psychological Trauma: Healing from Trauma and Moving On," HelpGuide, updated October 2018, https://www.helpguide.org/articles/ptsd-trauma/coping-with-emotional-and-psychological-trauma.htm.

17 Rachel Despres, "Signs and Symptoms of Psychological Trauma," ActiveBeat, accessed October 22, 2018, https://www.activebeat.com/your-health/6-signs-and-symptoms-of-psychological-trauma.

Chapter 5

1 "Causes of Trauma," Mental Health Connection of Tarrant County, accessed October 22, 2018, http://www.recognizetrauma.org/causes.php.

2 "Different Types of Wounds," Wound Care Centers, accessed October 22, 2018, https://www.woundcarecenters.org/article/wound-basics/different-types-of-wounds.

3 Abuse Wiki, s.v. "Penetrating trauma," accessed October 22, 2018, http://abuse.wikia.com/wiki/Penetrating_trauma.

4 Freyd, DePrince, & Zurbriggen, updated 2001, http://citeseerx.ist.psu.edu/viewdoc/download?doi=10.1.1.493.8095&rep=rep1&type=pdf.

5 "Trauma, Attachment, and Stress Disorders: Rethinking and Reworking Developmental Issues," HealingResources.info, accessed October 22, 2018, http://www.healingresources.info/trauma_attachment_stress_disorders.htm.

Chapter 6

1 ACE Pyramid Atlanta, Georgia: Centers for Disease Control and Prevention, National Center for Injury Prevention and Control, Division of Violence Prevention.

2 "Enlisting in God's Army," Back to Basics, accessed October 22, 2018, http://lhfbacktobasics.weebly.com/702-enlisting-in-gods-army.html

Chapter 7

1 Merriam-Webster online, s.v. "Bruise," accessed March 10, 2018, https://www.merriam-webster.com/dictionary/bruise.

2 Dr. Angie Panos, "Healing from Shame Associated with Trauma," Gift From Within - PTSD Resources for Survivors and Caregivers, accessed March 4, 2019, http://www.giftfromwithin.org/html/healing.html.

3 "Typical negative core beliefs," Balance Your Core Beliefs, accessed March 4, 2019, http://www.core-beliefs-balance.com/page33.html.

4 E. S. Kubany and S. B. Watson, "Guilt: Elaboration of a Multidimensional Model," *The Psychological Record* (2003), 53.

5 Sabrina J. Stotz, Thomas Elbert, Veronika Müller, and Maggie Schauer, "The relationship between trauma, shame, and guilt: findings from a community-based study of refugee minors in Germany," PMC, published June 22, 2015, https://www.ncbi.nlm.nih.gov/pmc/articles/PMC4478074/.

6 June Tangney, Patricia E. Wagner, Deborah Hill-Barlow, Donna E. Marschall, and Richard Gramzow, (1996). "Relation of Shame and Guilt to Constructive Versus Destructive Responses to Anger Across the Lifespan," *Journal of Personality and Social Psychology*. 70. 797-809. 10.1037/0022-3514.70.4.797.

7 Merriam-Webster online, s.v. "Shame," accessed March 4, 2019, https://www.merriam-webster.com/dictionary/shame.

8 Alex Korb, Ph.D., The Upward Spiral: Using Neuroscience to Reverse the Course of Depression, One Small Change at a Time (Oakland, CA: New Harbinger, 2015),

9 Karee Steward, "The Paralysing Impact of Shame: Resilience and Vulnerability of Refugee Youth," accessed October 22, 2018, http://www.murdoch.edu.au/School-of-Psychology-and-Exercise-Science/_document/Research-Results/2015-210.pdf.

10 Ibid.

11 Kathy, "7 Differences Between Shame and Guilt," Soaring Heart Counseling, August 21, 2012, http://soaringheartcounseling.com/2012/08/7-differences-between-shame-and-guilt.

Chapter 8

1 *Baker's Evangelical Dictionary of Biblical Theology* online, s.v. "Deliver," access March 5, 2019, https://www.biblestudytools.com/dictionaries/bakers-evangelical-dictionary/deliver.html.

2 Mimi Silbert, "Treatment of Prostitution Victims of Sexual Abuse," *Victims of Sexual Aggression* (van Nostrand Reinhold, 1984).

3 Temple of Ascending Flame, "The Four Angels of Prostitution," accessed March 5, 2019, http://ascendingflame.com/PDF/The%20Four%20Angels%20of%20Prostitution.pdf.

4 "Strongholds," GreatBibleStudy.com, accessed October 22, 2018, http://www.greatbiblestudy.com/strongholds.php.

5 "What does the Bible say about deliverance?" Got Questions, access accessed October 22, 2018, https://www.gotquestions.org/deliverance.html.

6 "Strongholds," GreatBibleStudy.com

7 Accessed March 5, 2019, https://www.coursehero.com/file/p4o4pt2/5-Jesus-never-commissioned-anyone-to-preach-the-Gospel-without-also-commanding.

8 L. R. Shelton, "Biblical Repentance/The Meaning of Repentance," Gospel Translations, http://gospeltranslations.org/wiki/Biblical_Repentance/The_Meaning_of_Repentance.

9 Accessed October 22, 2018, https://catnipblog.com/tag/creating-intentions-setting-goals.

Chapter 9

1 "How is energy distributed around the body?" r/askscience, accessed October 22, 2018, https://www.reddit.com/r/askscience/comments/38dbpm/how_is_energy_distributed_around_the_body/.

2 "Welcome Connector . . . this is your story," Mindtime, accessed October 22, 2018, https://www.mindtime.com/archetypes/connector/.

3   Pawel Olczyk, Łukasz Mencner, and Katarzyna Komosinska-Vassev, "The Role of the Extracellular Matrix Components in Cutaneous Wound Healing," updated March 17, 2014, Hindawi, https://www.hindawi.com/journals/bmri/2014/747584/.

4   "Wound Healing and the Immune System," accessed October 22, 2018, https://www.sitn.hms.harvard.edu/flash/2013/issue133a.

5   Kendra Cherry, "Extrinsic vs. Intrinsic Motivation: What's the Difference?" updated October 19, 2018, https://www.verywellmind.com/differences-between-extrinsic-and-intrinsic-motivation-2795384.

6   D. J. Leaper and K. G. Harding, *Wounds: Biology and Management* (Oxford: Oxford University Press, 1998).

7   J. Hutchinson, "The Wound Programme," Centre for Medical Education: Dundee.[Telci, Dilek, and Martin Griffin. "Tissue Transglutaminase (TG2) – A Wound Response Enzyme." Frontiers in Bioscience, 1 Jan. 2006. Web. 18 Dec. 2012. http://www.bioscience.org/2006/v11/af/1843/fulltext.asp?bframe=figures.htm

8   Ibid.

9   Ibid.

10 Leaper and Harding, *Wounds*.

11 Ibid.

12 "What is healing?" Quora, accessed October 22, 2018, https://www.quora.com/What-is-healing.

13 Leaper and Harding, *Wounds*.

14 Bessel A van der Kolk and Onno van der Hart, "The intrusive past: The flexibility of memory and the engraving of trauma," ResearchGate, accessed October 22, 2018, https://www.researchgate.net/publication/304347531_The_intrusive_past_The_flexibility_of_memory_and_the_engraving_of_trauma.

15 P. L. Dobkin, Ph.D., "Fostering healing through mindfulness in the context of medical practice," PMC, March 16, 2009, https://www.ncbi.nlm.nih.gov/pmc/articles/PMC2669230/.

16 Wikipedia, s.v. "Healing," March 2, 2019, https://en.wikipedia.org/wiki/Healing.

17 Michael Schmid, "Narrative memory and the impact of trauma on individuals with reference to one short sequence from 'Memento,'" Term paper (Munich, 2004), GRIN Verlag, https://www.grin.com/document/66502

18 "Creating new neural pathways," True Vitality, accessed March 7, 2019, http://www.truevitality.com.au/articles/creating-new-neural-pathways-2/.

19 "How Does Writing Affect Your Brain?" NeuroRelay, August 7, 2013, http://neurorelay.com/2013/08/07/how-does-writing-affect-your-brain/

Chapter 10

1. "Creating new neural pathways," True Vitality, accessed October 22, 2018, http://www.truevitality.com.au/articles/creating-new-neural-pathways-2/.

2. Ibid.

3. "Dr. Dweck's discovery of fixed and growth mindsets have shaped our understanding of learning," MindsetWorks, accessed October 22, 2018, https://www.mindsetworks.com/science/.

4. Phillippa Lally, Cornelia H. M van Jaarsveld, Henry W. W. Pottos, Jane Wardle, "How are habits formed: Modelling habit formation in the real world," European Journal of Social Psychology, July 16, 2009, https://doi.org/10.1002/ejsp.674.

5. "What is Brain Plasticity?" BrainHQ, accessed October 22, 2018, https://www.brainhq.com/brain-resources/brain-plasticity/what-is-brain-plasticity.

6. Deann Ware, Ph.D., "Neurons that Fire Together Wire Together," dailyshoring.com, accessed March 5, 2019, http://www.dailyshoring.com/neurons-that-fire-together-wire-together/.

7. Lynn Blumberg, "Neurotheology: What happens to the brain during spiritual experiences?" The Atlantic, July 4, 2018, https://www.sott.net/article/391062-Neurotheology-What-happens-to-the-brain-during-spiritual-experiences.

8. Ware, "Neurons that Fire Together."

9. Ibid.

Chapter 11

1. Alex Korb Ph.D., *The Upward Spiral: Using Neuroscience to Reverse the Course of Depression, One Small Change at a Time* (Oakland, CA: New Harbinger, 2015).

www.ingramcontent.com/pod-product-compliance
Lightning Source LLC
Chambersburg PA
CBHW071210070526
44584CB00019B/2980